I0762681

RESPONSES • KAFKA'S PRAGUE

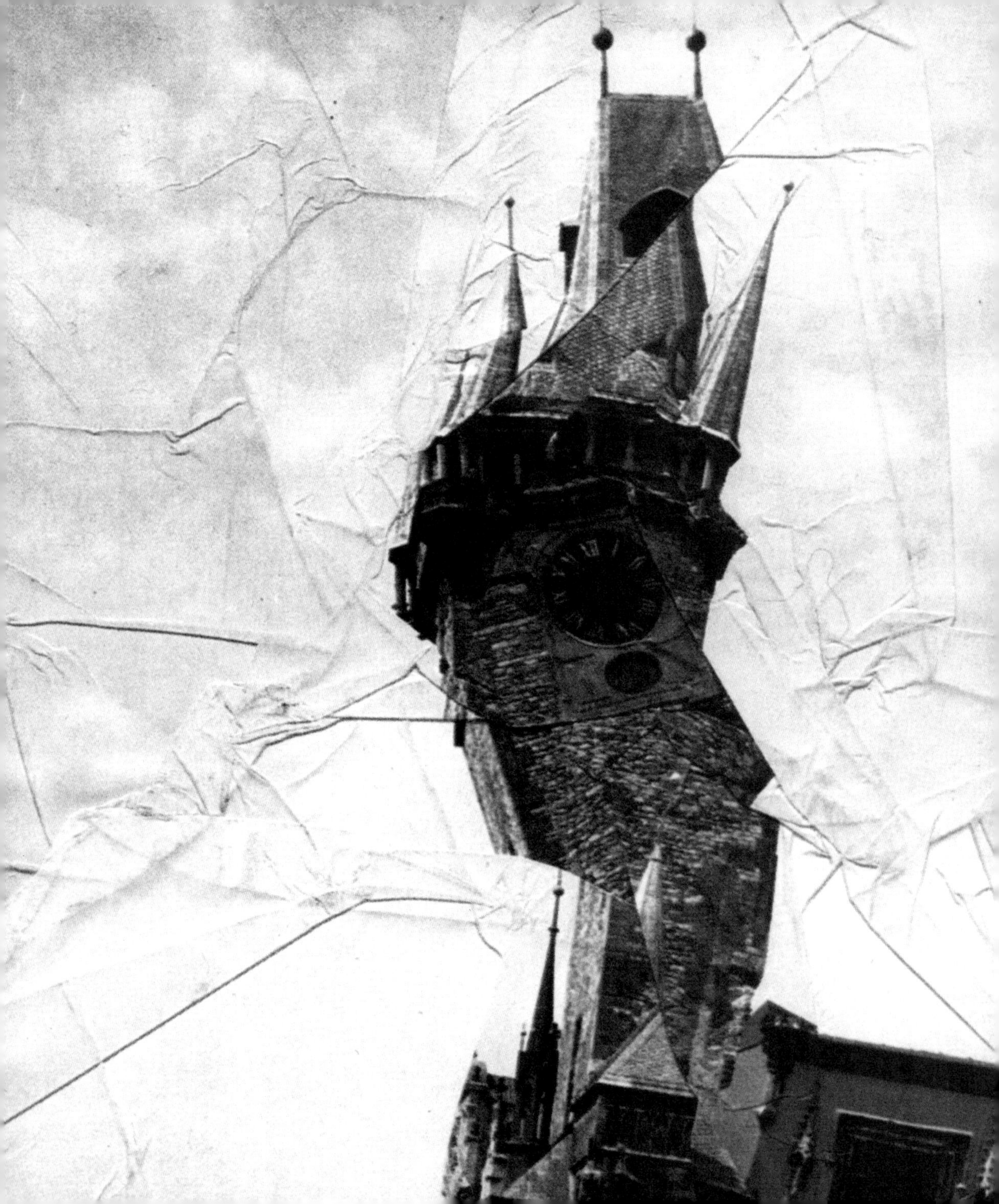

Jiří Kolář

RESPONSES • KAFKA'S PRAGUE

Translated from the Czech by Ryan Scott

TWISTED SPOON PRESS
PRAGUE
2021

ISBN 978-80-86264-57-8

The translation and publication of this book was made possible by a grant from the Ministry of Culture of the Czech Republic.

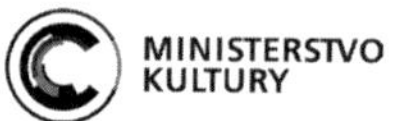

CONTENTS

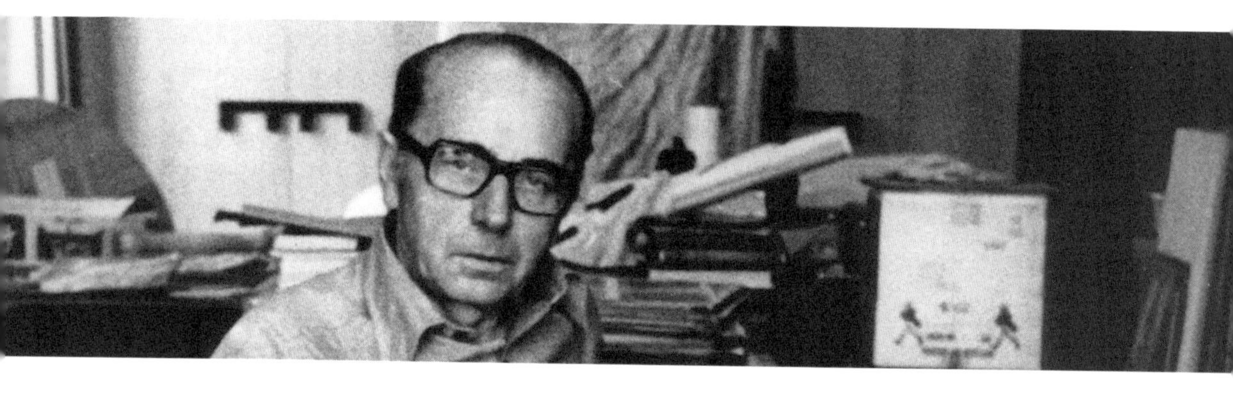

RESPONSES

In memory of Jiří Padrta

Art continues to evolve in its daily discovery of the world as part of the general drive toward universal knowledge — no matter the field involved, e.g., science, etc. For this reason, nothing arbitrary, no extrinsic new departure or approach, belongs to art, only departures and approaches already innate to it. Just as with science, where nothing may begin on its own but only when it's inherently part of things themselves (e.g., mathematics). It always depends of course on how things progress. Without this, no creative approach makes any sense. So nothing completely new can ever really be invented.

•

As in science, every new discovery in art broadens the field of human perception and understanding. This noetic aspect is paramount to me, and it also applies to all aesthetic concepts of so-called beauty. If beauty attains perfection, then the aesthetic scope of understanding is generally broadened. If art posits a new worldview, then the scope of human understanding is generally broadened. A beautiful portrait can still be painted even today — yet Leonardo perfected it. Van Dyck consummated this perfection so that ultimately a new direction was required. Rembrandt abandoned all idealization. Picasso enriched his painting through the inspiration of African art, children's drawings, etc.

•

If art by art alone is to expand human consciousness, then no type of endeavor should be foreign to it. Being blinkered severely impedes this expansion and may actually be regressive, regardless of direction, even if forward. Having blinkers on perhaps is useful in times of crisis — and since crisis seems to be a permanent condition, all art in our era is in a way crisis art — if it doesn't act to retard despite all the boldness and discoveries. I would be skeptical of it. In fact, it appears to be more against than for humanity. Maybe such questions aren't useful for the individual artist who couldn't care less, but the fact is, without them I can no longer think. Yet art per se isn't nonsense, on the contrary, it's amazing just how necessary and useful it is for understanding the situation of humanity today. And its importance cannot be overstated. Art and poetry don't necessarily result from the expansion of consciousness but are actually produced through the process of this expansion. A poem, picture, etc., always wants to enthrall, and this is ultimately the intention of any artistic fixation, whose intensity and breadth determine its fruits. Even for poetry the law applies that if one type of art is no longer sufficient as a means of expression, or if a different outlook can be imagined — it should never be called superfluous. Far from it, because right at that time, right at that moment, it is indispensable for a new way of thinking, a new way of expressing. There needs to be more than a single mode of creation today for ample progress to occur. This is absolutely necessary, and this necessity is the very proof of the present inadequacy. A given mode of creation is pioneering only so long as it doesn't presume to claim that it's impossible to make progress without it.

•

My interest from the beginning has been to locate the points of friction between visual art and literature. Up to now all such attempts have seemed to me devoid of scope and largely lacking in rigor. Even though significant advancements were made, by Marinetti for example, some of the old aesthetic remained underneath. The same holds true for Apollinaire. I find it interesting that what Mallarmé started in this regard other poets like Eliot picked up on, and with the *The Waste Land* — which I consider one of the greatest modernist poems — he created a de facto collage. In prose it was Joyce who had some influence on a particular poetic period of mine simply by the way he was able to handle the various aspects of realia in *Ulysses*, where he readily blended argot and the language of sentimental novels into a literary language.

•

The word "modern" is very old and has always been applied to those who come up with something new. More recently, it has been used for those who aren't afraid to experiment — those who've not only discovered a new, different reality, but also expressed it differently. And I think this all started in modern art and modern poetry. Poetry had to be done differently. To my mind true poets are those who actually write. A multiplicity of aspects and disciplines is understandable and typical for today. I don't like to prophesy because all prophets, including those of such status as Dostoevsky, come off as foolish. Even so, I readily admit that I expect a new art to emerge that will likely have very little in common with the art of today. It will offer a different perspective, undoubtedly needing time to crystallize, but in the form of an entirely new discipline. It won't be poetry, painting, or sculpture, but perhaps something quite different. I cannot even say what right now. Maybe someone will find new relationships between the various disciplines of modern art — as presently exists between linguistics and biology — and connect all of this one day in a new system. I don't mean to say a poet will emerge who will comprehend everything, but whoever it is will definitely have to feel and be able to perceive everything. Poetry isn't just a type of special poetic understanding or a type of language, it's a special type of perception as well. In art, a person has to be attuned to specific ways of perceiving. There are many people the world over who have no capacity for this or anything of the kind, it simply is beyond their grasp. It is a type of enthrallment and curiosity. The more dulled this sensibility, the lesser the poet. This is why Joyce attempted to create an all-encompassing character, complete from all perspectives, not omitting the most banal acts, such as shaving, and including relations as remote as reminiscences are for Homer. So what we call new art today is likewise attempting a similar polymorphous unity of aspects, methods, and disciplines.

•

It would seem that experimentation and daring in art presents more a danger to wrongheaded people than anything else. Start to think for yourself and you are more dangerous than anything that can be made. The truth is, all the power of art and literature largely comes from its ability to produce a shift to a new field of perception. If most of literature has really been used until now to enslave humanity, it's likely because this stage of its development corresponds to the same stage of a humankind still unable to stamp out war and hunger. When the army barrack takes priority over the hospital. Unfortunately, I have to throw schools into the same bag with barracks, with hospitals I can't add anything except cafeterias.

•

Writers take such a great interest in the world because everything is a mystery to them. And since it is their duty to unravel this mystery, they select certain authors who match their destiny and expand their field of perception. For one poet to be able to expand the field of perception of another, he must learn from those who are expanding it toward other disciplines, whether in art, science, philosophy, or other fields.

•

Einstein didn't visit Picasso's exhibitions for no reason. And art isn't discussed among some of today's leading lights in academia for no reason, just as they don't discuss religion and mythology for no reason. Usually it's even one of their main interests — to decipher the mystery of humanity. I like authors who are dissatisfied with how things have historically been investigated and go right to a place to see for themselves, like Levi-Strauss going into the field to find out the truth.

When I started to dismember verse, I had to obtain material on the origins of writing in general. This led me to create petroglyphs and knot poems, for example, the inspiration coming directly from such original research. Though history has taken these phenomena into account, they weren't ascribed any role in the development of poetics. Because at the same time all this is part of the history of poetics, and as such remains alive, just as Altamira remains alive for modern art.

•

Why do poets keep returning to their childhood as the most blissful age? I didn't find it so blissful. I have rather embarrassing memories of my youth and would prefer never to talk about them. My happiest time was between the ages of 35 and 40, and maybe up to 50, when I started to have some sense and when the world along with experience began to become not necessarily more open to me, but clearer. When I started to realize what was going on. The rest were just impulses I already had inside me — just an apparatus I'd been operating, just a basis for metaphor, for stylizing something. Poems weren't my only means. The point was to grasp and express humankind and its destiny in all their flux. Because a person changes moment to moment. When I began to make poems for the blind and crazygrammes,* serious poets, whom I had believed understood a thing or two, didn't want to understand me at all: Poems for the blind and lunatics? But to create a poem for the blind so they could recognize an abstract image, what an abstract poem is from touch, not just from being told what it is but on their own, this was more important to me than a description or explanation of what an abstract painting looked like.

•

*Poems for the blind were made by punching points into a sheet of white paper to create a low relief that could then be read by sight or touch. Derived from Apollinaire's *Calligrammes*, crazygrammes are collaged illegible writing as if done by someone mentally disturbed or so traumatized the ability to write has been lost. [All footnotes are the translator's.]

I think every artist one day must, like it or not, try to effect what's called a revolution: a reshaping and reinvention of poetry as a whole — as in my case — no matter its current relevance, major or minor. This is entirely the poet's own business, just as it was my own business. No one demanded anything of me, and no one was interested in anything of the sort in my work either. But I felt I had to make a radical change, that I had to risk it. This required enormous commitment on my part. But such a step can only be taken with great deliberation and foresight and with a healthy dose of — strangely enough — hypocrisy toward oneself. Otherwise it founders. Why do I say "hypocrisy"? It comes from Baudelaire: "Hypocrite reader — fellowman — my twin."*

Baudelaire in fact knew that when he wrote he had to be hypocritical toward himself. That as soon as he failed to be, such that someone could chastise him for a mistake, he was finished. A poet must have certainty and expunge his work of all vulnerability. Naturally everything is vulnerable in the end, but it's incumbent not to make yourself wide open to attack. When I began to try my hand at writing poetry, I hardly knew what was going on elsewhere in the world. Later when I saw the great collections of Kupka and Kandinsky for the first time, it was a crushing realization for me that these artistic feats had been achieved by the year I was born. So what was I supposed to do? Yet I had already created a bit of work by then, and apart from other things I had an inner need to push my work further.

•

*Charles Baudelaire "To the Reader," in *Flowers of Evil*, trans. James McGowan, (Oxford: Oxford University Press, 1993).

It's imperative to appreciate poetry's historical development. Every attempt at change and revolution came out of something. In my case it was the experience of modern American poetry, which I translated, along with a bit of the European poetic tradition. Consequently, one day it hit me that Apollinaire replaced the word with the picture and Breton with the object — but both were essentially old in the same way, both stood on the foundations of traditional poetics. Breton never made a whole verse, a complete poem, with objects, and you need to know French to know what word in the written text a thing is replacing. This was one of the first steps, albeit intuitively, toward a new poetry. Surrealists weren't thinking about the history of poetics in this regard, as they were too fascinated with their discoveries and then mainly with the fallibility of freedom. They conceived a freedom of creativity but forgot that it's governed by laws. They conceived an aesthetic freedom but applied it in such a way that an artist who was different wasn't merely an artist, a person, in their view, but someone who didn't understand art at all and a minor villain because he didn't write like a Surrealist. And this has actually persisted to this day.

While such intolerance might be understandable, it amounted to one of the greatest misdeeds in modern art. I get that Breton couldn't accept a Mondrian, but it begs the question: which of the two accomplished more? Some regard Mondrian as a marvel because his paintings depicted the world as order and he didn't want to make it more awful than it already was. For me, it was crucial to discover who was right, the one who saw man as an apparition from Dante's Hell or the one who saw the world — as did Mondrian — as this great orderly structure with roots reaching back to Giotto's *Descent from the Cross.*

•

I'm in no way disparaging Surrealism. Yet there are poets who travel their own path. The kind who observe the world and prefer not to comment on it. Since often it's impossible to do so. There are moments when it becomes necessary to construct the world on purity — such as with Mondrian — while also foreseeing its imminent horrors — as is said of the Surrealists. In my opinion, they didn't get too close to this, they laid the "psyche" on too thick. After all, the horror lay in its simplicity. Concentration camps were something so horrifyingly simple and inhuman that it's impossible to talk about them. No one has surpassed Bosch's method of painting nightmare. Maybe only Dalí has come close . . . Just as there was a grand, affirmative, inviolable purity among the constructivists, it is a shortcoming of the Surrealists that black humor was the only response they could muster. That they were unable to demonstrate that humor could also be pure. They were too committed to the unconscious, which in their view was black. But the unconscious may also be white, just as love is white. Surrealists kept talking about love, but for them it was more about genitalia and morbidity, and quite often they conflated absurdity with morbidity. In some of its new iterations, e.g., as part of contemporary happenings, this morbidity is often naïve and repulsive.

•

The Parnassianism and Artificialism present in most of the available European poetry hit me the hardest during those early war years when Nazism was on the march. At this time I returned to Arnošt Vaněček's translations of American poetry — and I was swept away! For much of that period, the years when one's perception of the world is the most intense and pure, I was living in Kladno, in an apartment overlooking the steelworks, the blast furnaces, where the glow of the molten slag poured by the smelters lit up the whole night. When I first read Sandburg, under the sway of this scenery, he at once became my native poet. The transformations of men at that time into outlaws brought me closer to Edgar Lee Masters, and I even called him then the new Ovid, author of a new *Metamorphoses*. He taught me to take notice of human destinies, the destiny of each and every person I met. He taught me to see, hear, and feel differently, as if he had transformed all my senses. And because I had admired Whitman since I was a boy, I dove into his polyphony and almost drowned in it.

•

I was never the kind of poet who surrendered to moods or a worldview. I had to grapple with them. Dante felt no compunction about cramming all his enemies into Hell and all the people and things he felt some affection for into Purgatory, where they would still suffer — and those he truly loved he put in Paradise. Although he's the one inquiring, he answers himself why they've been consigned to Hell. He isn't impartial. You can only side with your own conscience. And a limited outlook, intelligence, connection to the world (and I had none at that time) will land you in your own personal jail. You make your own jail, your own darkness — and have to break free once more. One day you become convinced it's time to let it go, that you'll be burrowing in the prison of your own solitude to the day you die without getting anywhere.

Eventually I realized that the world isn't a concentration camp at all. "What I raise up causes someone's fall — what I drop will let them soar," — once wrote František Halas — and this contradiction always comes to the poet over the years. He has to accept that this is where he lives, and even though people were imprisoned in concentration camps, they might've been beautifully in love and happy elsewhere. To love while knowing he's surrounded by the despondent: this is a terrible thing for a poet. But since he's aware of it, they are simply creatures who love or suffer. There is a difference between a person and a creature. A person sees the world's contradictions and understands that in fortune and misfortune the world also contains goodness and love. A creature is one-dimensional, only interested in football or cars and sees nothing beyond that.

•

From the beginning my ideal way of working has been not to persist in something once discovered. Not to be a craftsman of a single work. Artists post-Joyce must be interested in everything and realize that the history of the world commands them to do things differently — and to flee from what they already know how to do.

•

It keeps occurring to me that the element of meditation has vanished from art, that the work of art has completely stopped being a reason for meditation and has largely become a game. In other words, I think the poets for whom the meditative element was the basis for all their work were the ones responsible for its very dissipation. What seems to have won out is the element of discourse, even if a discourse of conflict, zero-sum, where either my opponent wins or I do.

I think that an artwork or poem could result from contemplation, just as contemplation could be achieved in the process of making a work, or the overall tenor of a work. Yet any work created by a method lacking contemplation is utterly inconceivable. Everything depends on it. I think contemplation is the very process of working, and what's important — as scientists say — is not making something, figuring something out, but how the work is done. What this *how* brings into being is another question.

Clearly each era has its own method of contemplation for a given type of work. The salient point is that though results may be achieved by different types of contemplation, it's always through doing the work. Contemplation may thus be of a different type and order and applicable in different creative fields. When two poets write a poem on the same topic, different types of approaches and contemplation are brought to bear. Contemplation, however, is indispensable. And there is one more thing: the artwork itself as the object of contemplation. I know what I do, but do not know, or have to find out, what I actually did. You think you're doing something, but only once it's done can you reflect upon what you actually did.

•

The material itself gives you a chance to think differently. But it's through contemplation that you're able to avail yourself of this chance. Pollock had to work out the possibilities of drip painting for himself, that the technique itself, i.e., dripping, or choice of material, in his case, house paint, gave him the chance to broaden the field of perception.

•

It seems to me that despite all the rancor and noise, it will always hold true for the artist that what's important is not the result but the work and the effort expended. What is produced astounds and inspires, but the effort it took, the difficulties overcome, the exertion, hardship, and sacrifice all serve as an example. And there can never be too much of it, even for epigones.

I don't want to sound like I'm griping about epigones. A genuinely committed epigone knows what creative work is. He is a seeker. And under certain conditions this might be hugely significant. Especially for the consciousness of simple folk, within other traditions, in a new and different environment. Worst of all is that today these "quasi-artists" have died off and imitators in full gear have taken their place. Not only is nothing sacred to them, but they are capable, and often perfectly capable, of anything and know how to make everything. They present the greatest danger to modern art, those who vulgarize it like this, not those who oppose it on principle. That is, everything today has become modern — as conceived by those who are perfectly capable of adapting in the blink of an eye. Someone not well-informed will readily take what these imitators produce as real works of art.

So this is why I say that the time will come when it will be easier to tell who's a true artist. Imitators can't make heads or tails of real art. And yet we will always find them near its source and always at the front lines — though this might just be part and parcel of contemporary art.

•

I think that everything is essentially a product of the word. Whatever the word's origin or primal meaning, it started the first sentence, and thus language. There's a reason the Bible says: "In the beginning was the Word . . ." And I think language is irreplaceable. We have to distinguish expression from speech. As soon as humans understood this difference, the first verse, the first communication, and with it the first question perhaps then formed on their lips.

•

For the poet, language is a type of understanding as well as misunderstanding. And out of this misunderstanding — whereby something ensues that I will call a conflict and struggle with language — verse may emerge. This implies something other than ordinary speech, it implies something that will advance language — will enrich it.

We broaden the field of knowledge through language, clarify problems through speech. Either we clarify or obfuscate them. Such obfuscation might be why we started to think differently — just as clarification goes beyond what we knew before and how we knew it. So both may be progressive for the knowledge of language, which undeniably has its own history and evolution. Their current version seems to be a symptomatic linking of language with different perceptions and new concerns. New words are thus coined proportionate to new sensibilities.

•

Colloquial speech differs from poetic speech in somewhat the same way as a spring does from a faucet. Water flows from both, but speech is a sort of pure spring, while I can turn on a faucet when I want. I can drink whenever I feel like it or need to. The spring continuously flows and you can go to it any time, anyone can without having to do anything at all. It's the opposite for poets. They have to turn on the faucet. Someone or something in them turns on the faucet . . . Poetry is an art of language — Valéry once said — that is, as long as I'm not referring only to spoken language. Yet through it I understand everything that surrounds me. Since myriad things and events might speak to each one of us in a way other than directly by words. If we take language as something universal, that it isn't merely used as personal expression, that an event often affects us more palpably and powerfully than something written or spoken, that language is more than the uttered or written word, then I would have to agree with what Valéry said.

•

In Mallarmé's case, it's not about, as is sometimes claimed, breaking the rules of language, but a new crystallization and enactment of new rules for poetry. Mallarmé did something groundbreaking. He elevated form to content. It was the discovery of a new poetic perspective.

Marinetti's liberated word was then the first geyser, gushing onto ground mapped out by "A Throw of the Dice." The difference was that Marinetti still focused on literature, it was a genuine revolution of the word. Poems were to become spoken or verbal pictures. In contrast, Mallarmé was demanding it be music.

•

Calligrams are dangerously close to what we call "pouring new wine into old wineskins." But if Apollinaire had rediscovered and created them in such a way that his reader didn't need to understand French to have an idea of the poem's content at first glance, he would have taken a decisive step beyond Mallarmé.

•

I happened to be quite tired the first time I visited Ms. Guggenheim's museum. A strange saying popped into my head: "This new world is an ogre without the old one." In other words, to purge your mind of everything old — like the Dadaists did with the whole of their revolutionary gesture and newness of things that was their bailiwick — is undoubtedly a fallacy. I would even say that our experiences today draw more on the old than the new. The Surrealists made a futile attempt to disregard old artists who had expressed metaphorically what made them "surrealist." Dadaism as well finally started to notice that not everything could be rejected, that it wasn't possible to operate under the slogan that everything was only Dada. They inevitably had to take into account the method of great artists. So actually even they unwittingly leaned on tradition. Something that directly necessitates tradition just occurs in modern art anyway. Breton understood this very well.

•

I believe that Joyce and Eliot were more astute than all the Dadaists put together, even with Marinetti and Apollinaire thrown in. While it might seem at first they didn't do anything so radical and revolutionary, with respect to the intellectual side, which until then had been traditionally dominated by Poe, Baudelaire, and Mallarmé, these two were their greatest spiritual successors. And yet it's true that outwardly they weren't conducting any grand experiments on a revolutionary and radical scale. I, for one, am not against such gestures and experiments, for as Valéry stated, the laboratory is essential — just that the public doesn't always need to see it. (Although an atomic blast happens before the eyes of the public since it can hardly be hidden, its inception and substance are calculated in the laboratory. How odd that all this rests on a few lines of math by Albert Einstein.) If we consider Eliot in this respect — and I'm thinking of *The Waste Land* here — he created the first collage in literature, something that no one had ventured before him. No one had imagined connecting the past with the present and the future. Before he came along no one had realized that within the heart of each person the past communicates to an extent with the present, that it is capable of showing human life entirely anew. Joyce was dealing with the same thing. No wonder he said in an interview that he was fascinated by *The Odyssey* and wanted to show that a modern person could experience in one day what Homer's hero experienced over many years: and this was incredibly important as it was something for which earlier literature needed a more elaborate narrative, that each one of us is inherently an Odysseus who can experience our own great journey each day. Through what's encountered or isn't encountered even in that quietude when you only dream, sleep, or read, listen, see, and observe. That something magnificent takes place over a mere twenty-four hours.

•

Lettrism, letter pictures, visual images, let's choose the common term concrete poetry — and in the latest phase evident poetry* — possibly arose out of a need to convey a gesture. This gesture was to replace everything that could only be depicted or described, narrated at length, or told with the aid of numerous mechanical means. Consider, for example, gestures of contempt. They may be expressed by nodding the head, wrinkling the brow, raising the eyebrow, narrowing the eyes, smiling maliciously, jutting out the chin, a vague wave of the hand, twisting the body, crossing one leg over the other, etc. Any simple or complex sentence, or dozens of methods, can be expressed in the same way. A gesture occurs in a single instant, and only literature is capable of complex description or depiction. Only an actor or a film is capable of immediate expression. And now it's time for literature to step up! Text should be used as images — or snippets of text and fragments of images because modern printing enables and allows poets to say these things without having to describe and depict by traditional means. And it all had to fit on a rather small piece of paper. The Czech literary critic F.X. Šalda said: "A poem is will in a crucible." The method of concentration and condensation I have in mind required thinking about the poem differently than had thus far been the case to make depiction or description superfluous. This meant the field of perception had to be broadened without an old mode of writing, without old modes of speech. So poets sought and found new approaches. When I was making my punctualist poems, for example, I had to follow certain new rules and get to an endpoint — just as with punctualist, or pointillist, music, where only the

*The use of visual materials instead of words for poetic expression. According to Kolář: "It is all poetry that excludes the written word as the load bearer of creativity and communication."

beginning and end are prescribed and the musician has to choose how to play the music. This is allowed in the new modern poetry, in which, as I once said, the word should stay inside you and initiate an internal monologue. Didacticism falls away, that is, description (because today description is understood as didactic), which might be absolutely necessary for certain types of understanding of reality but not essential for poetic understanding. And it's especially unnecessary with modern communication technology. But paper is still paper, and a book a book, and if I want to impose these standards on them or in them as an author, as someone who writes, without substituting the film reel or tape recorder for them, I myself must find the most suitable mode of expression. So there is always a need for poetic work. Khlebnikov had to invent his own language for his poetic purposes. Called Zaum, it was used to express his thoughts differently from ordinary language. Even though Khlebnikov still relied on Russian, his achievements in this area were considerable. Heisenbüttel chose the route of permutation. He knew that a single word might have multiple meanings. Based on how it's delivered, how it ripples out, how it pulls along substance and material associations, forming a chain. The visual poet needs images for this, yet is satisfied with a single phrase that can be dismantled and jumbled in permutations. In this way polysemy is created — or a polyphonic signification of one intent, of a single expression. One more poet should be included here — Christian Morgenstern with his great humor. He was one of the first major poets who thought about the essence of speech — he invented the language of fish. He was in fact the first evident poet — a mighty revolution indeed.

•

All artists create their own secret language, similar to what a child does. A child does it unconsciously, the artist with the whole force of his being. When we fold a page, tear it, or cover it, nonsensical, decontextualized words emerge at random. This operation in itself is not the poet's objective. It is something else, the disruption of organic energies! Here I would like to return to Khlebnikov, who was one of the first to realize that a word is charged with a powerful energy. That certain clusters of words represent powerful fields of energy, one pole of which is in the person. When it collides with another, the external pole of a word, an electrical charge is sparked. Given that Khlebnikov also knew that any simple or compound sentence, speech, greeting, dozens of moods could be uttered, he therefore ranks among a few major precursors who not only sought out new modes of writing but whose thinking was more occupied with how to write and how to express. In the first instance, when writing was the primary issue, typographic poetry was created. Generally its only impact was in showing that the variously sized letters available in the type case could be imbued with something intuitive or ideational.

•

From the very beginning I have felt an affinity for those poets who were dissatisfied with the status quo in poetry. This actually all started with Mallarmé. Schwitters and others followed in his footsteps, so that I could adopt aesthetic principles with the mindset of someone who wanted to take it further, go further in a certain direction, further in a certain type and method of work and expression. Without a critical attitude, skepticism, and artistic prescience, without the burden of experience — I'm thinking here about those who came before me — nothing at all can be achieved. The poet must absolutely appropriate everything that strengthens and toughens identity — even if it's something given and uttered, or never attempted until now. Above all, you have to be observant, and have willpower. To discover what a sentence conceals and not believe only the first words. This I suppose was the goal. After a discovery is made, you work independently, following your own will because it's in thrall to the power of the work being created. Just like all poets of my generation, I had reasons aplenty not to trust existing poetry, old forms of writing, even if the most exquisite. I'd rather not come out against Valéry here . . .

•

When you have a fateful encounter, you generally have to communicate in some way other than merely with words. To react with serenity, silence, and gestures. Just like Mallarmé, who employed music, I knew that a fateful encounter also allows for silence or an accentuated singularity in words, sentences, and poetry. From the outset I realized that the prevailing music of a verse was simply inadequate, that even the most beautiful verse was a Parnassian product, no matter how audacious the content. My ear at once became attuned only to ordinary spoken language. I went to church to hear the prayers, I became conversant with the drone of machinery and the din of the crowd. But what interested me was not so much originality as their richness, their fullness, as a natural, commonplace phenomenon — and if all this could be regenerated. I thought: "To chance upon something. Anywhere, anytime, anything — that's the thing." And I often repeated to myself: "When you truly stumble across something, it's just a scale. Now you have to give it a go. Play!"

•

I felt the need to reevaluate language not only in terms of the stilted, outdated, traditional persistence of its symbolic meanings, but through the lens of the work done by modern music. I found only a few poets who realized how wide the chasm between poetry and music had become. They might have learned to tackle anecdotal content, yet for the vast majority of them form remained a total taboo — even for Surrealism. Maybe only Breton gave it some thought, but hardly anyone else outside of him.

•

For me the destruction of poetic language followed the same path and the same type of perception as did a new and different type of perception in other disciplines. As I've already said, this is primarily the case in music and the visual arts. I was speaking about a type of perception — what I mean is that I couldn't keep seeking poetry in the written word, I had to go beyond the written word. It meant finding another, living language.

•

Certain laws and axioms articulated by major philosophers persist in the same way as a beautiful poem or a wise saying persist. I could add that I've always repeated anything I've done: to make commonplace what was exotic, complex, to distill what was naïve and simple and airy — and to resurrect what seemed dead. To make what was discordant and drab, unparalleled and, if I may, the marvelous; to make what was bloodless, exciting; to make the taciturn, cheerful, etc. — and — vice versa. Above all, the intensity of every perception, or even only an impression, had to be ratcheted up. I wasn't generalizing how susceptible the evasive spirit usually is to this. I had to take a path different from anyone's before me. Or only with those who pointed out my path.

•

My collection of urban folklore was created in collisions and constant encounters with what I have called sources of inspiration. What was considered living folklore before me, I stopped recognizing as living long ago. So I surveyed my surroundings, and when I did, I realized how inexhaustible the old folklore was. Yet I also couldn't afford to close my eyes and not hear or see what was forming right before me and what I had to hear right at that moment. This made me, unwittingly and profoundly, happy. This was true in my quest for those sources of inspiration. When the finds accumulated, when there were more of them, I saw that the work had in fact been done by nameless people who consequently created something in the modern era alongside the advent of modern art that was just as original as the old folklore. This new one was peculiar in that it was only really emerging in big cities. It could be found in magazines, originating with factory workers who were not leading a traditional way of life like country-folk. I saved these found sources of inspiration, though I only started to work with them in a deliberate way after the war. My friend the writer Zdeněk Urbánek, for example, discovered the possibilities of rapportage.* We both immersed ourselves in it and realized that

*A simple juxtaposition of two or more unrelated, unaltered images to reveal a particular relationship between them.

collage had to advance further, across the mighty river engendered by Ernst's work and style. We weren't afraid of imitation and didn't want to create new artistic symbols and myths, nor any sort of intricate or fantastic illustration or dream. Reality was closer to us. The chief objective was to make a "short circuit," an immediate connection, tangible. Our advantage: we weren't visual artists. We didn't want to imitate but make something without the intervention of scissors and utility knife.

•

Having a model is only one factor in accomplishing something, even something substantial. It might also provide the impulse for immediate future work. Even the mere mention of what someone else is doing might be an influence on you . . .

•

If I were to discuss the principle of identity, I would have to talk about the relationships between everything I've experienced and done. These connections have escaped me until now, and I had to locate them somewhere for me to actualize this identification in the processes that so deeply interest me. So for me the work of art became a kind of fount for expressing certain impulses and their combinations — even if I hadn't anticipated anything artistic to come out of the process itself.

•

Simply stated, I came to the realization that not only the substance of engravings but also the majority of reproductions, and anything actually, is imbued with a considerable poetic charge when prepared in a particular way. For this reason I started to work with material different from what Ernst used, for instance.

•

My first prewar collages were still under the sway of Surrealism. I was quite young and interested at that time in the chance encounters doing such work brings.

•

Doesn't literature to some extent serve to enslave people? And weren't the major works of the past exposing the fetters of that enslavement? Don't we call some people slaves to their passions and don't nations today still strive to enslave their express symbols — hasn't literature served this purpose to this day? Levi-Straus, for example, has already accused literature of serving society's repressive power. I think that some major artists found a way to avoid this. Such as Shakespeare, Dante, etc. From today's perspective, however, even Dante's work bears the traces of an intellectual enslavement to religion. It is certainly different from the Aristotelian principle of freedom. If it is true that almost all literature has served oppression, then the new literature can be viewed as furnishing an alternative — showing the what and where of this oppression. All of this will last as long as it takes for individual disciplines to split from one another emphatically and decisively, just as it is necessary today to unify or at least tie together these art forms so that one cannot be whole without another. It would be like being born without arms or legs, without even realizing or wanting to admit it. All it takes today for someone to be considered a genius is to entertain this viability and the symbiosis of one art with another.

•

Establishing new relations between whatever interests us, what brings us life or is thrown in our path by chance, prompts on its own the urge to write — though nothing is harder because everything that seems over and done with is quite often the most open and accessible. I mean a work we had considered closed, finished. Yet to me Dante is open, as is Shakespeare, or Bach. Each major work of art that seems absolutely finished in reality offers more inspiration and stimulation and paths to follow than may seem apparent. All of these major figures are in fact inspirational. Their works, done long ago, continue to radiate tremendous inspirational energy for the genuine poet.

•

I discovered there's nothing at all unnatural about the mythologized Surrealist loci of chance encounters, but it is somewhere different for every human destiny. It is only a matter of recognizing the energies that create chance for a given fate. Someone disposed to trust the power of their thoughts, in which the Surrealists excelled, is capable of accomplishing much that is admirable and rare. Many Surrealists undoubtedly did. Dalí in his early period, Ernst in his frottages, collages, and in many paintings, Breton in his discoveries . . .

•

At the risk of oversimplification, I would say the question of how to replace color and structure, and with what, sparked the development of Cubist collage. For Surrealist collage it was how to draw and create a sleepless dream, whereas the Dadaists dared to disregard color, structure, and drawing. Ultimately even dream. They knew how to work with paper as an element and material in its own right. The best Dadaist collages were made from the ephemera of the most modern civilization of that time, meaning from reproductions taken in hand daily, from newspapers, magazines, and photographs of everyday life. The Dadaists did not shy away from reality, it seemed to be the very place where they sought the meaning of their revolt. While the first Schwitters collages might have communicated something quite different, we shouldn't forget his discovery of collage in relief — Arp as well. Nor should we forget that grandiose idea of building the Merzhaus. Schwitters was the first malcontent. And also the first to create a work of art in which he was a component himself, in which he could actually live, work, and continue to add to whenever he wanted. Compared to this work some recently created environments strike me not only as spaces crammed with a wide assortment of post-Surrealist and pseudo-Dadaist detritus but also as an unbridled game, which has largely left me cold. Only a few were brave enough to go further, and for the most part they were kinetic artists.

•

So many circumstances hem you in that you have no choice but to consider how a given constraint might be exploited. Was it a coincidence that I didn't have the means to do my work better or differently? I made do with what I had and discovered in secondhand bookshops — or with what was given me. Was it a coincidence that the painters Karel Malich or Robert Piesen, or other friends, gave me the most beautiful reproductions from their archives? Was it a coincidence that Bohouš Hrabal was baling wastepaper for work and perfectly understood what I wanted to do and provided me with piles of material? If these are coincidences, then coincidences are a part of life, just as dream is a part of sleep.

•

I said before that I didn't feel as if tearing, crumpling, and cutting reproductions and texts were acts of destruction. It felt more like a kind of interrogation, as though I were constantly querying something, or something were querying me. I asked myself: What was beyond the page, the letters, the picture, inside all of it? I knew something had to be there. I felt like a strange anatomist or biologist. A word, sentence, poem, or page might have its own independent existence, and like a person's existence it might be very profound, and maybe even more profound without some of its appendages, such could also be the case with a poem. A picture as well. The torsos of old sculptures are testament to this. Just a fragment is enough to glean something about the artist. This explanation verges on the didactic since the poem or the page have to be worked above all. And this work is acutely merciless. Perhaps it's a form of mania, but Balzac's emendations and Dostoevsky's manuscripts always excited me more than the printed book. All of it affected me more powerfully than the actual reading of the work. The main thing for me was to get inside the author. I was always more interested in the process than the outcome — the final version. I felt like an apprentice observing how his master works.

•

I felt it important that my work be anatomical rather than destructive, albeit only in the theoretical sense. Leonardo had to cut open his first cadaver in order to see the lay of the muscles inside. I had to cut open a word in order to see how it was composed. Biologists didn't know how a living organism developed or how it functioned until the microscope became available, until they managed to differentiate red and white blood cells. I also needed to know the composition of a word's blood cells. To me this path leads to birth and not to destruction — a path to germination. Anyone in a state of arousal may observe this germination in themselves. An artist feels this "altered state," this arousal, constantly. So what they write may be and is different in each poem. It is only the intonation of thought. The poems may be nearly the same, but each one has something completely different to tell. They might be pictures — like with Braque — just slightly shifted, but each one now has something else to say. When I was starting out, I recall confronting the question of how someone illiterate would write a poem. How would it be done by someone who only knew a knot alphabet, petroglyphs, etc. This *how* haunted me and gave me the courage to take it further. Of course later I was able to say goodbye to all this. I already had it all in me and didn't need to search for any self-abasement, which comes while working all the same — figuratively speaking it meant "carne-vale!" — farewell to flesh! I was now governed by a different self, a different spirit. The spirit I summoned by everything my brain would allow me to do in the next moment . . .

•

At one time I was convinced that each poem should have its own particular form. I wrote in a way to express and reinforce this awareness. This idea hounded me for a long time, even as I started to make evident poetry. In one phase the evident intelligibility of a poem actually began to elude me, especially with crazygrammes and object, visual, or color poems. Without a tangible fixed order, the results were too chaotic, something that was more collage, or a confused form of it, than a poem. So I used a system of rows as a specific form of expression. Apparently they were comprehensible, as a knot poem in a horizontal position was comprehensible, even if arranged on the board in the most convoluted way. Knot and razor poems were to be positioned horizontally in the trial phase. I find it interesting, and in this respect characteristic, that some of my visual and circle poems from lips, eyes, fingers, etc. didn't impress anyone on their own. Yet the moment I incorporated them into a narrative whole there was overwhelming interest. Something had to remain, a row had to be retained. People had found it incomprehensible enough when I wanted to make my object and visual poems into free verse. When I wanted to choose a different form, collage was the only option. I had to return to classic linear expression, one verse following another, with stunning colors even assuming the role of rhyming in several visual and picture poems. This new type of perception, not of reading, is what I was after.

•

Anamorphoses were known long before my time. Many knew how to tear up photographs and experiment with the fragments before I came around. One of my friends who knew I was interested in this type of experimentation brought me a small collection from England that contained cut-up photographs assembled into rather evocative form. This only confirmed for me the possibilities of a new type of collage. I had an auspicious idea when I began: to use reproductions instead of photographs, and rather than at random, cut into strips precisely measuring a centimeter. It wasn't my intention to make these collages and rollages* myself, as I was convinced this was best left to the professional artist. Yet something was nagging me not to just dismiss out of hand what I was carrying inside me. So I went ahead and made a few of these first stripped collages. But when I proposed this new technique to several of my painter friends, it was met with such a lack of interest that I decided to continue on my own. For the rollage there are no rules except to cut and paste in place as precisely as possible. The selection of material is dictated by what I come across or manage to hunt down. Sometimes I'm immediately able to see the elements of humor, symbolism, or beauty in a collage, at other times I don't notice at first, or become aware of them a long time after the work is finished. I admit that the humorous aspect often interests me more than anything else. Perhaps this is why I find the work itself fun and enjoy doing it. I would be happy if others also found it amusing.

•

*Made by cutting two or more identical reproductions into equal strips and then mounting them in altered sequence.

Over time it occurred to me that the black humor of the Surrealists found in a majority of their past work, including Ernst's collages, is somehow fading away. These works have presumably become more poetry than they were originally. Only yesterday I was looking at an Ernst set in an exhibition catalog, and it seemed utterly devoid of black humor to me. It had simply vanished. The work was merely beautiful, and it was poetry.

•

When we look at a stranger, we see his figure, his face. If we start to converse with him and learn his life story, then this might interest us more than the face. So while everything may seem apparent in outline, there's always something else still. The contours of a person are filled in according to who is looking and how well the subject is known. The same applies to any item, any destiny, any story. A particular configuration of words may appear astonishing to us until we know its history. Unless we penetrate the history of an idea, a poem. Until we know who created it and when. The history of thought and poetry isn't static, it evolves. Otherwise, we wouldn't be able to progress in what we're doing either.

•

Prollage* has the ancillary title of Magrittage for the simple reason

*Made by cutting out a shape while leaving the contours, a cow or goose or birds, for example, and then inserting within that outline a different image to produce a visual silhouette similar to some of Magritte's paintings.

that René Magritte was the one who discovered it — I only swapped a brush for a blade.

•

It seems to me I was always doing the exact opposite of what the *nouveaux réalistes* were doing — even though I sincerely admire their work.

Duchamp and Christo gave a new meaning to commercial art. During Duchamp's youth the whole world, especially America, was inundated with traveling salesmen showing their wares from a sample case. This is perhaps the original impulse for Duchamp's *La Boîte-en-Valise*. This implies, in my estimation, that it was an idea typical for America.

Christo elevated window dressing to a new type of art. I believe if there were no factories he'd have to be content with collage and demonstrate what he was all about through painting.

•

Stratifia* were never meant to be pictures because the philosophy behind it, as I once defined it, was to help me discover how many revealed and hidden layers we have inside us. Look at how much we have to discard. How deep we have to probe ourselves — to be authentic when doing anything vital. And, conversely, how many ideas, how many disguises and masks we have to don where our consciousness rebels. Life, however, is in charge!

*Made by cutting through multiple layers of paper of varying colors and shapes pasted together.

•

Every writer knows what it's like to write three or four verses of text and then crumple it up and toss it into the trash. One time when I did this and wound a fresh sheet of paper into the typewriter, I wondered if the first draft of what I wanted to write — the discarded one — should be scrapped after all. When I fished it out of the trash and straightened it out a little, it flashed through my mind what the text was missing — namely, creases. As though spellbound, I tore the blank paper from the typewriter and crumpled it up, and the creases remained after I smoothed it out: In front of me I had a blank sheet of paper with an unknown writing scrawled over it. Perhaps an infirm writing, perhaps of rage. But more than anything it was beautiful, and that's how it started. I used a white sheet of paper at first, then black ones, letters, notes, engravings, and reproductions. Crumplage doesn't work all that well with dry paper. It has to be properly moistened and the work done quickly. Crumpling must be done fast and carefully, and it's difficult to predict results with this technique because it's always the brother of chance. Because the moist paper is crumpled and the work has to be finished fast, hardly any adjusting can be done. Its meaning can be demonstrated on yourself, in that I think each one of us is burdened by countless moments when something has collapsed and we have to get on with our lives, even if reluctantly — don't we all live with something broken inside? Maybe what's inside us or in whomever sings again, sings even better — can we then say with any certainty that destruction doesn't represent the beginning of something new?

•

My depth poems came about after the stratifia, but more or less concurrent with my first experiments with depth collages. The very first was a depth magazine poem. Yet the elementary impulse was a torn page from the "Homage to Kazimir Malevich" section of *Silent Poems,* my collection of concrete poetry. At the time I was under the spell of a kind of "anatomical passion," whereby I felt the need to dissect everything. Just as newer and newer layers are revealed in stratifia, with repeated readings of an image we discover something new each time. In other words, we penetrate ever deeper into it. The same goes for music or poetry. I wanted to give this a specific expression. So I folded over and layered on top of one another pages with different writing or images inscribed or pasted on them and then perforated it to make the depths visible.

•

I wrote poems as if the moment before their creation were like the moment before the creation of a piece of music. I knew from my process of writing what sorts of things surge into a person's head when the pen is lifted or the typewriter tapped. Capturing this state was my goal then — first and foremost. I should point out that I knew Strzemiński's work and his theory of Unism, which had a huge influence on me. I always felt galvanized by the composition of feathers, the arrangement of scales, when stroking a bird or fish. Walking on fallen leaves and their arrangement on the ground.

The fact that no one in art had dared to do something similar from a single material led me to the first chiasmage.* I attempted it

*A collage made from a large number of torn or cut-up fragments taken from printed or handwritten text, regardless of language, and then pasted together to form patterns and shapes, sometimes in low relief.

and was astounded by the result — I'd made the first monochromatic collage!

•

I wrote a musical score named for Baudelaire* because the majority of sound poets didn't know how to express themselves other than as cabaret artists. Only a few of them managed to surpass the Dadaists, such that almost all of their magnetic tape has seemed to me merely a recording of their own recital, or more precisely, of a recital of their "products." From the outset I had Mallarmé in mind. Perhaps in him lay the starting point and solution: to make poetry through music — to write a musical score for a recital — for the recitation of a single word! Obviously I cannot deny the influence of specific music, especially several Americans and others in this age of contemporary musical experimentation. The image suddenly wanted to be read anew and, moreover, heard. Most musical compositions require ensembles and a conductor to interpret them — I was working with this objective in mind.

Pummy, a man with an electric brain who should survive a thousand fatal accidents. This is the fate of each work of art. Each month, before each spectator, before each and every critique, to remain untouched, or to survive!

•

*In 1963, Kolář created a series of 23 "sound poetry scores," he named *Hommage à Baudelaire*, which look like concrete poetry images. Later combined with other techniques such as crumplage, chiasmage, etc., his "musical scores" were collages of notes written on a staff that were then superimposed or replaced, deformed and defaced, so that the notes would be reconstituted in different form.

The need for a plasticity of letters, always treated formally otherwise, imposed itself on the process. At the time I jotted down several notes about this: artists shouldn't be afraid to use whatever means to achieve their vision. Anyone who might think this (as applied by me) too bold should be aware that for me it's a matter of what's available at the moment and not what I would use if I had other options. An artist compromises his ideal rather than pushing its boundaries . . .

•

I wrote poems to make readers confront themselves. Or I left them the freedom and space for their own participation. My evidence objects compelled them to observe sections from various angles that could only be seen when a certain part of the object was turned, or themselves in it as if in a mirror when it was either raised or manipulated in some other way. More than just being a game, I wanted to force the viewer to react, to engage in activity, even though the object was self-contained even without any such action.

•

The first time I encountered an advertising poem, I was flummoxed, and I confess to being tempted to write something similar. When I read it to Bohouš Hrabal, he told me he felt the same immediacy from reading cookbooks. The roots of what I later called destatic poetry, or "action poems," can be located somewhere here. I noticed that from the time we're young each of us is surrounded and bombarded by instructions. The ingenious part is that we are supposed to do one thing in order to do another. Take a cookbook. First I have to light the stove, then put the water on, next take certain ingredients and work with them. Only afterward does something quite different emerge — a meal. Or let's look at alchemical literature. What a plethora of different instructions and processes! And no one reached their goal, whether the philosophers' stone or the elixir of life. Alchemists, for example, used prayers to measure time, not to mention other methods. But with poems it's a little different. The process is as important as the outcome. And this applies to destatic poetry as well — and could be said about happenings, too. Destatic poetry is, however, the diametric opposite. Anyone who would conclude that I run the risk of displaying the same kind of exhibitionism as the creators of happenings is mistaken. Destatic poetry is not meant to produce amazement or any other form of manipulation, but should serve instead to provoke the most piercing, rigorous observation of oneself, of one's mind and spirit. Just as we all listen to music, read, love, eat, etc., how we want and when we want, so destatic poetry, in how I conceive it, doesn't prescribe anything other than what is written. If I'm to say something about the ritual aspect of destatic poetry, then I would have to stress that I generally favor only religious ritual and human dignity. To repeat, my intention was to create something that should be more than read, so that what we call poetry could be felt. And mostly so that coincidence could be actualized by all. Perhaps I don't have the right to speak this way — but in truth the word wasn't enough for me. I felt it were charged with an energy different from what had thus far been utilized.

Each poem, picture, composition, sculpture assumes a viewer, listener, or reader, as does a play. So for my *A User's Manual* I assumed performance.

•

I've always been interested in magazines and newspapers, not only in their forms, but everything about them, especially in the postwar period when I got a thrill out of everything on all those pages! The very fact that it's practically impossible to print a newspaper even a day in advance! This unpredictability was my main incentive to start keeping a diary. I had to observe what was going on, and not only in the world at large but right around me. And what was going on not only around me, but also in me and how I would learn to deal with it. My first attempts at a diary were in poetry and prose. The subsequent motivation to make diaristic collages came from a similar place and distanced me even more from the principle of old collage since I could no longer work in this way. Time determined the *what,* and the *how* more often than not came from this *what*. For example, Japan influenced me in an entirely different way than America did, events in Paris differently than those in Prague. And all this elicited the need for a different formal handling of surface. I found the work beautiful and gripping. The primary ingredient for a diary is how events affect you. You buy a variety of admission tickets and fares, all sorts of things are purchased, letters arrive daily, perhaps a death notice among them. You can never know what a day might bring. When you bring it all together, you compartmentalize the items on the surface by way of compositional intuition guided by experience. And I called this array evidence poetry. This unpredictability of what the day would bring had the actual nature of a witness to my day.

•

Just as thousands of events enter our lives, they also go away and disappear, leaving behind something that seemed insignificant to us before. I was often surprised that something like a detail had stuck in my memory, and even more often I was always more interested in the technical side. How the thing was written down or fabricated. For a painting, it was always more about the composition than the story. It never occurred to me to be interested in the story of a Pollock painting over how he made his paintings.

•

I became familiar with so-called Mec Art while working on several exhibition projects an architect friend had asked me to do. I'm grateful his confidence in my work put a degree of certainty in my hand, and in particular he helped me to try out many things in dimensions that had otherwise been completely out of reach for me. I could extend a rollage to 30 meters in one exhibition! His support allowed me to easily determine what is megalomaniacal and what is truly monumental when creating large pieces.

•

I enjoy working with print and paper that have been marked by time, especially when marked by the live touch of human hands and human involvement. My best crumplages were created from reproductions that readers had colored themselves. All of us know how many traces human hands leave in books.

•

Form or content becomes trivial when we fail to notice the hidden meaning. This is as true for art as it is for nature and the universe overall. I couldn't even say if a single one of my works has a trivial form, and as for content, I've been talking about new perception going on ten years and dogged by the term "new consciousness" to boot. This does not imply that I'm attempting to do something pointless — a futility beyond all futility. The art critic Jindřich Chalupecký was well aware of this eternal battle against the void. Given that he discussed the silence behind my work, I should be grateful for the metaphor, which condemned my work to be at one with the human universe.

•

In art, one thing has the same value as another. The surface of a Seurat painting is as important in the center as in any of the corners. In Czech, the word for "factualness" is related to "being matter-of-fact," or "impartial." I would like my things to be interpreted in this way.

I am intrigued above all by how things impact a person and a person things. For me, the point was to divorce things from their conventional symbolic schema. This symbol-generating con nauseated me more than anything else. Everything became loaded with symbols, and yet everything had already lost meaning before them. Although this has lasted for several millennia, we always embrace the same things, seemingly unable to shake free of them. This is precisely why it will be so hard to transform the world. This is precisely why the purity of things was mentioned, that things cannot be freighted with symbols. They must be left as they are. Otherwise all sorts of truly arbitrary action might occur, such as Freudians claiming a tie may symbolize (even if only as a substitute) a noose or even represent genitalia — which is utter nonsense. I'm not saying this has no place in art, but as for myself, I understand such approaches as arbitrary and have always been against them.

•

Is it possible to imagine a craftsman without a connection to his tools? Whoever has such paltry personal experience easily believes that people genuinely dislike using any tool other than the one their hand is used to. For something from their blood and their life has flowed into these implements. Just as so much of your life creeps into things such that you're able to recognize them among dozens of the same, even after a very long time.

If I weren't convinced that things have their own destinies, independent of people, I wouldn't be able to write a single authentic poem. Doesn't some war photography relegate every poem about Vietnam somewhere far beyond the work of even the worst local newsperson? Something such as a report may never, of course, completely replace the testimony of a poet. It is only one possibility when looking for meaning in life. It is only one phase of a type of perception, with which I qualify any artistic process in general.

•

My former found objects were left unaltered, they were simply found poems. They are objects revealing their uncommon destiny, that is, they radiate poetry.

•

Yet I wasn't only excited by things, but also by the sight of construction sites, factory floors, and train stations. The same goes for peering into the window of a living room, the guts of an appliance, eternity. All of this captivates me more than ninety-nine percent of modern art. I experience a similar thrill when entering a new unfamiliar environment, seeing for the first time a huge computer with its housing removed, its insides exposed. This was actually the case at the time I was starting to make my first confrontages.* All this always energized me more than a painting or a picture could.

•

I had the sensation of being surrounded, for example, in natural history museums. Later in museums in general, whether technical, ethnographic, or whatever. Imagine me as a young boy in the museum, and all the birds, fish, and animals I'd never seen up close were congregated there in one fell swoop. I suppose my present loves and interests began somewhere there. Anyone who has ever visited a large museum anywhere in the world couldn't avoid being awestruck by the history of nature, or the history of the human spirit, or simply the human spirit in general. I'm not talking about books and libraries. I've never understood those folks who thought to disparage these institutions as being obsolete, deserving to be destroyed — I've simply taken them for idiots. It's just bombast, like with the Futurists. I

*The juxtaposition of at least two photographs or reproductions showing similar actions or gestures yet occurring in different milieus and performed by different figures.

know they get annoyed at everything connected to tradition and old culture, but an artist must be clearheaded above all. Though all sorts of things might also be created out of silliness, much of what is requires substantial modification.

•

I haven't been hurt in life by the aggressiveness of things as much as by people's incapacity to learn, which emanates from a surfeit of stupidity that still has most of the world in its grip and manipulates a large part of humanity. A person is manipulated by specific social classes, no matter if a caste of the wealthy or of politicians. And both my plays, *Our Daily Bread* (1949) and *Plague in Athens* (1961), took direct aim at this reality, with which a free person never had any truck. I didn't write these dramas under the force of some slogan of alienation. I don't think ordinary people are to blame for this modern word's meaning as much as those who control and oppress them do. For me, Samuel Beckett is the greatest spirit of our age. And with his first one-act plays Ionesco touched the heights reached by Chaplin and the whole golden age of American slapstick. For he recognized that a word knows how to rejoice even in our day, and what's more — he understood the anatomy of laughter. What I've said presupposes knowledge of their work, which I've translated into Czech. And there is something else both have forgotten: namely, that not even their plays have moved the needle much since the time of Shakespeare. Despite all his deep internal polyphony, Beckett could manage just fine within the framework of drama established by Shakespeare. And Ionesco eventually fell into the didacticism of Molière.

What was engendered in literature then — let's recall the discovery of Heißenbüttel's first permutations, the first experiments of Franz Mon, not to mention what took place in Paris, Vienna, or America etc. — wasn't the spawn of literature alone but bubbled up out of the ferment common to all artistic fields. I didn't care if I could write something better but if I could construct what I did write differently — on the basis of a new principle. Even back then I called both my plays theatrical collages. Please don't confuse this with montage. Many playwrights and directors have worked with montage. I call it collage because only it could dislodge fable from the stage, only it could provide the fullest polyphonic range, as the cornerstone of a new type of play.

•

Every single thing that comes into our lives is colored by our fate. The deeper our understanding of a thing, the more it has intervened in our lives. Things also live and grow old with us, and are always dependent on how we live, what we live, what changes mark our lives. I'm a writer, and I know how to read the destinies of things. Once I even tried to read what lay in store for new things, with whom they'll commune, what their future will be — and one day I had the urge to make this script of scars and human contact visible. So this is how I began to paste things together, my poetry — objects. Picasso was the first modern artist who felt the human essence of things, as though he believed they were sentient. This was how he was able to say wise and beautiful words on his love for things and on the coexistence of things in his paintings. He was the first to understand that things can speak to each other. Suddenly, you notice that some things get along and some don't. And you need to have what doesn't get along around you a long time before you get used to them, and they to you and to each other. It's a special kind of mysticism, but that's the way it goes. You have to develop a relationship to things, and through this it's as if they begin to click on their own.

•

At the beginning of the 1950s, the photographer Eva Fuková and I were working on the idea of how things come to an end. Not only are thousands of people dying every second, but millions of things are, too. Some die slowly, others lightning fast. Others outlive their fate in pieces, and I think a good study or even a book could be written on this. Having to relearn everything from the beginning after my stroke in 1970 also forced me to learn to think anew. What often required my stubborn persistence and what had been hard for me to work out now was coming to me all at once on its own. The past merged with the present, fiction with reality, fantasy with consciousness. All of it with especial intensity. I returned back to the time when I didn't regard a thing as something exceptional, remarkable, and a tree, house, flower, stone, sun, chair, thought, etc. at once became familiar. I could speak familiarly to them, as if we were friends, tell them off, love or fear them. Time was one, space had no dimension for me, and I saw practically without perspective, upside down, as if something proliferating and chaotic. This was exactly how I thought and felt at this time. Just as every country I visited would captivate me with its terrible beauty, hope, and freedom, now I felt a similar kind of hypersensitivity toward everything. What I've always striven for I will never lose now. It is the belief in the immense oneness of reality.

Because my unreal state was also reality. I started to learn how to work. This meant how to hold a pen, tear off a piece of paper, speak. I felt my own proliferation and decay. That is, I was able to observe myself. My head suddenly filled the whole room. My limbs grew into the yonder. Everything fell on me in gargantuan dimensions.

And perhaps the one we call God, whom I also call God, heard my pleas. I cannot say this any other way. What followed? My work was liberated from everything that ever could have hampered it. I never felt so free. If I've ever been afraid of not being able to complete something, I am no longer. I can now say precisely what I felt — and I am more free. I know that I am mad, but isn't this whole dangerous world mad? And does it make any sense? I think it makes no difference: I'm open to everything. The fact that I'm still alive implies at least some sense. That's why I'm open to everything.

Prague – Paris, 1973

KAFKA'S PRAGUE
(1977-78)

Translated from German by Kevin Blahut

1

Was soll ich tun? oder: Wozu soll ich es tun? sind keine Fragen dieser Gegenden.

Die Acht Oktavhefte

"What should I do?" or "Why should I do it?" are not questions that are asked in these regions.

The Eight Octavo Notebooks

St. Vitus Cathedral ☞

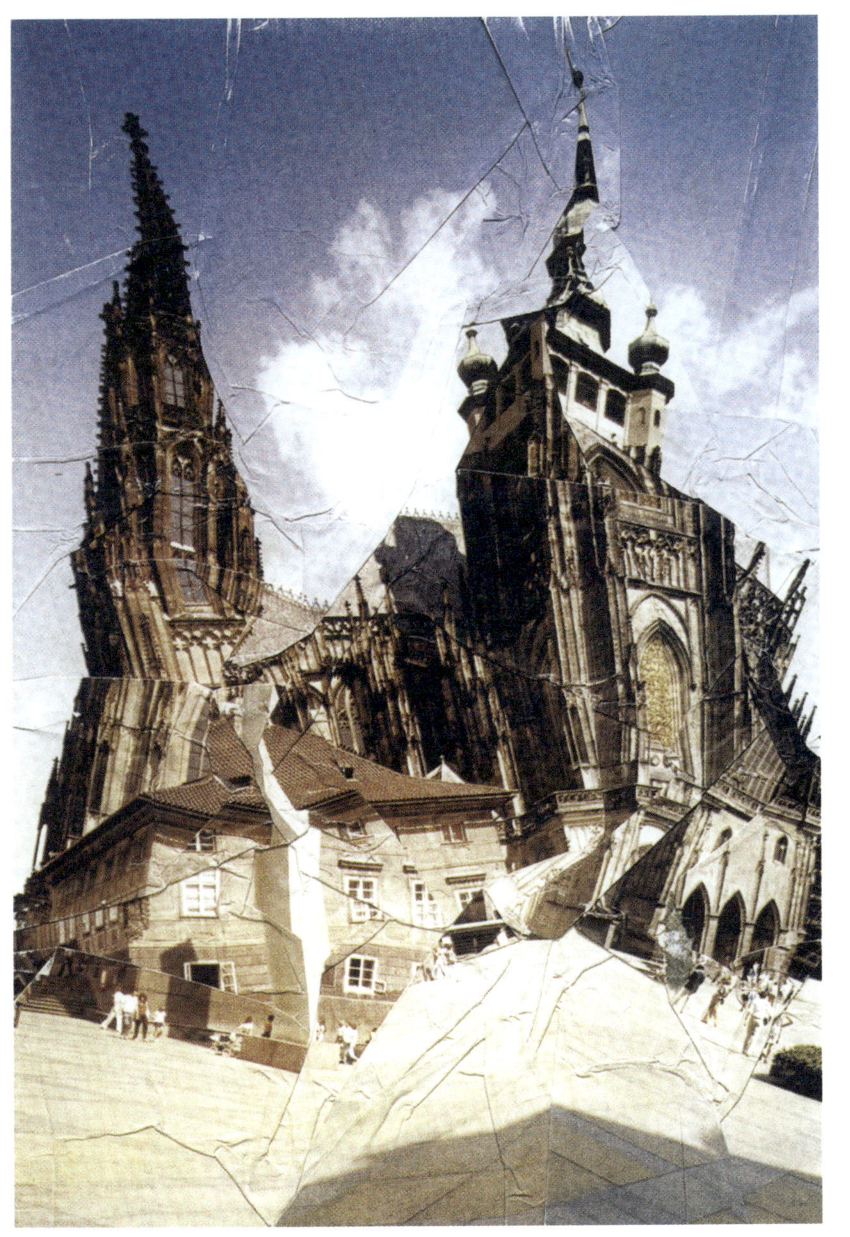

2

... etwas Irrsinniges hatte das — mit einem söller-artigen Abschluß, dessen Mauerzinnen unsicher, unregelmäßig, brüchig wie von ängstlicher oder nachlässiger Kinderhand gezeichnet sich in den blauen Himmel zackten.

Das Schloß

... it had something insane about it — concluding with something like a balcony, whose battlements stood jaggedly against the blue sky uncertainly, irregularly, friably, as though drawn by the hand of an anxious or careless child.

The Castle

Prague Castle ☞

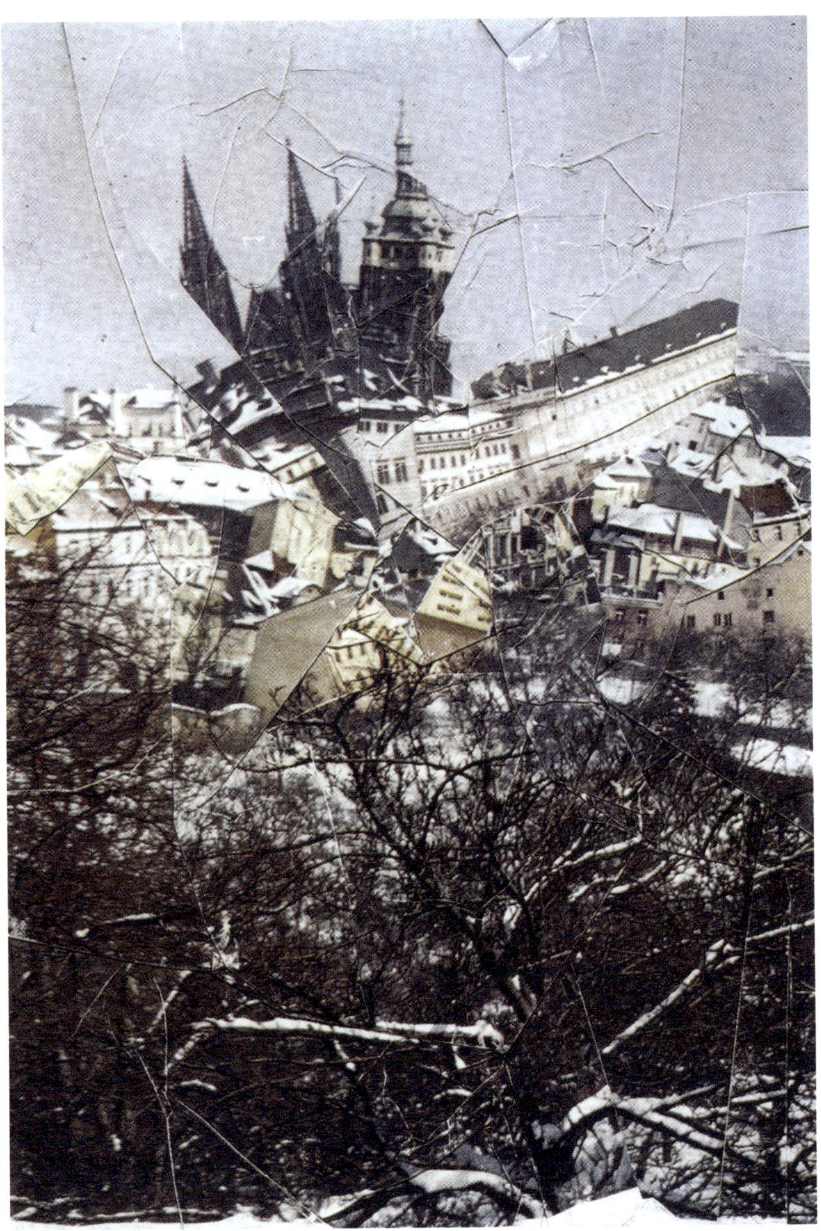

3

Es ist sehr gut denkbar, daß die Herrlichkeit des Lebens um jeden und immer in ihrer ganzen Fülle bereit liegt, aber verhängt, in der Tiefe, unsichtbar, sehr weit.

Tagebücher

It is quite possible that the magnificence of life lies ready around one, and always in its complete fullness, but covered, in the depths, invisible, very far off.

The Diaries

New Town Hall ☞

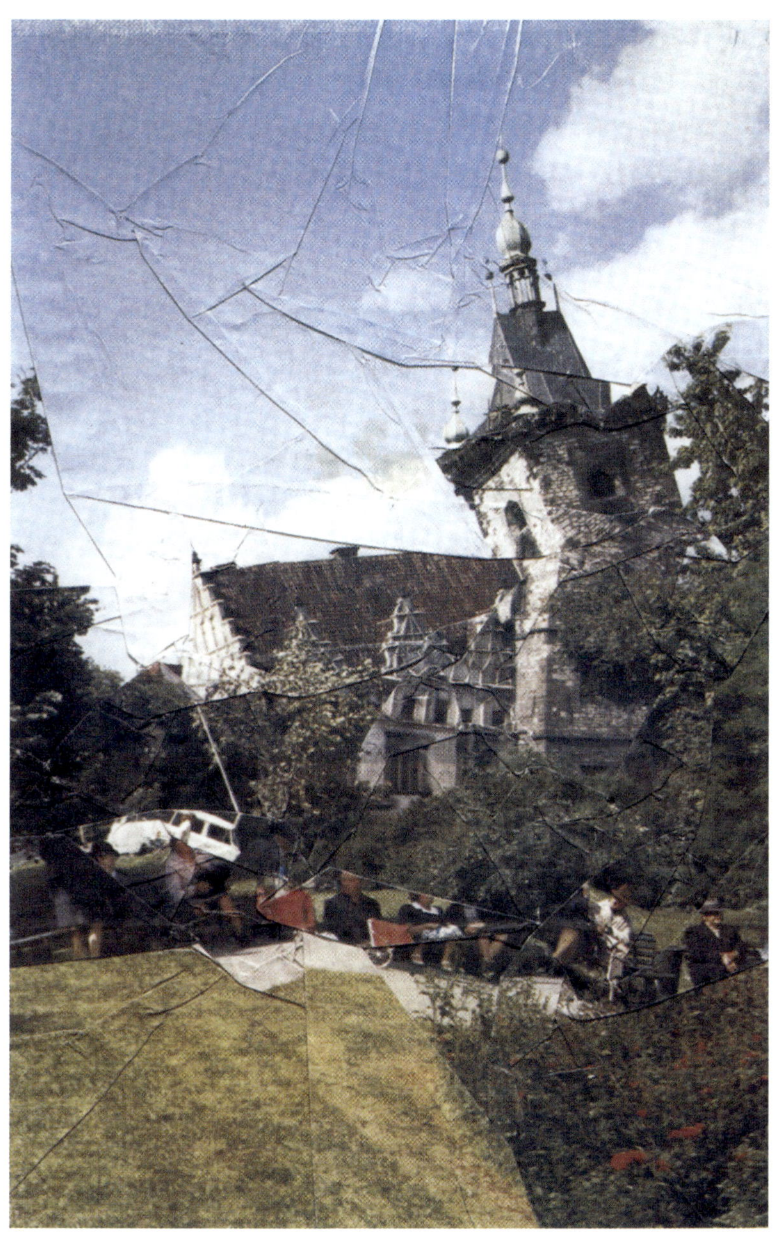

4

Als wichtigster oder als reizvollster ergab sich der Wunsch, eine Ansicht des Lebens zu gewinnen . . . , in der das Leben zwar sein natürliches schweres Fallen und Steigen bewahre, aber gleichzeitig mit nicht minderer Deutlichkeit als ein Nichts, als ein Traum, als ein Schweben erkannt werde.

Tagebücher

The most important or the most appealing was the wish to gain a view of life . . . in which life retained its natural heavy falling and rising, but simultaneously was recognized with no less clarity than a nothingness, as a dream, as a floating.

The Diaries

Old Town Hall ☞

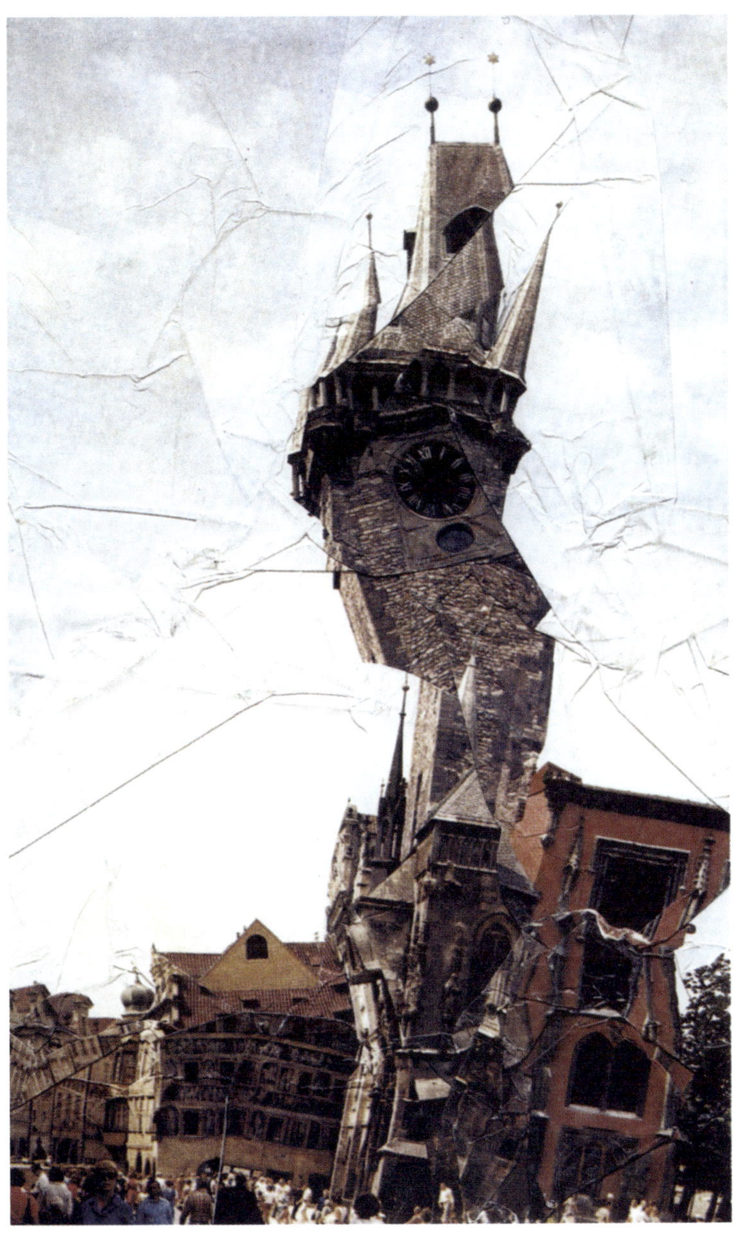

5

Dort drüben ist eine Angelegenheit der Nacht, durchaus in jedem Sinn Angelegenheit der Nacht . . .

Briefe an Milena

Over there is an affair of the night, certainly in every sense an affair of the night . . .

Letters to Milena

Mostecká Street ☞

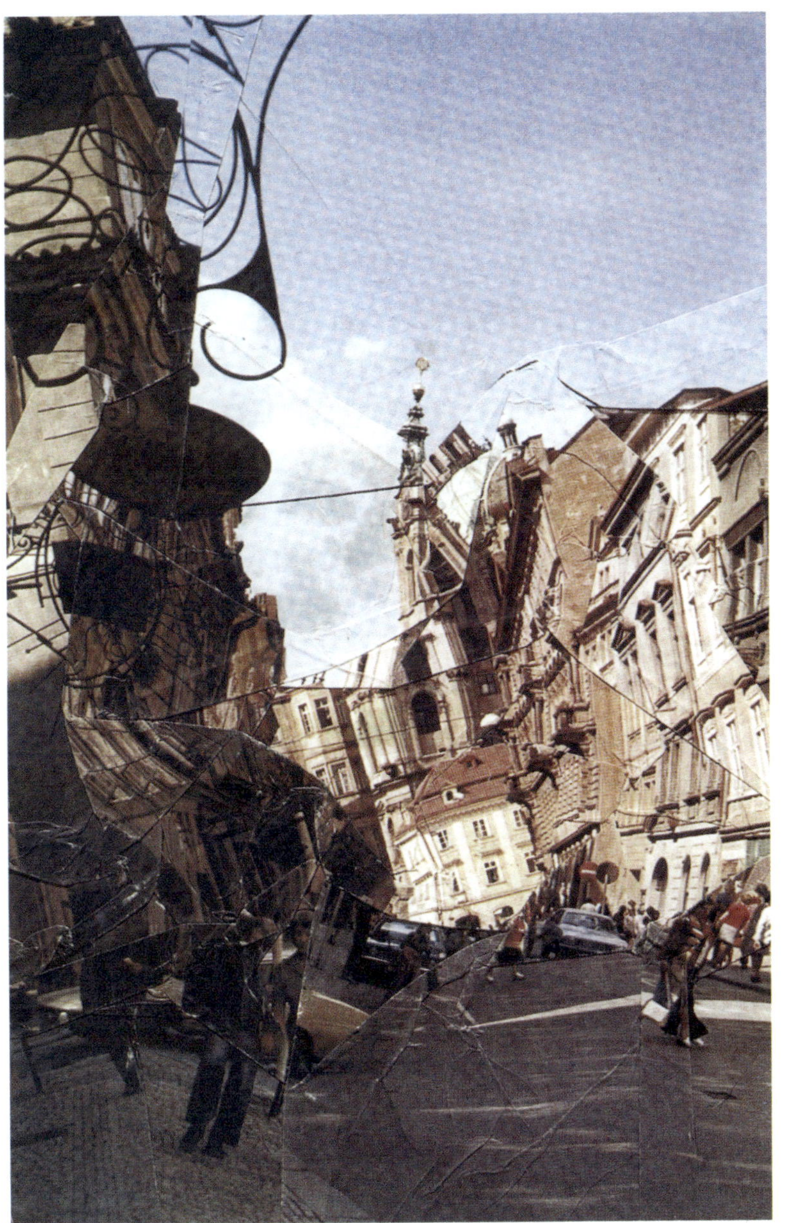

6

Hast Du also einen Weg begonnen, setze ihn fort, unter allen Umständen. Du kannst nur gewinnen, Du läufst keine Gefahr, vielleicht wirst Du am Ende abstürzen, hättest Du aber schon nach den ersten Schritten Dich zurückgewendet und wärest Du die Treppe hinuntergelaufen, wärest Du gleich am Anfang abgestürzt, und nicht vielleicht, sondern ganz gewiß.

»Fürsprecher«

If you have started on a path, continue on it, no matter what. You can only win, you run no risk, maybe at the end you will collapse, but if you had turned back after the first steps and run down the stairs, you would have collapsed right at the beginning, and not possibly, but quite certainly.

"Advocates"

Nerudova Street ☞

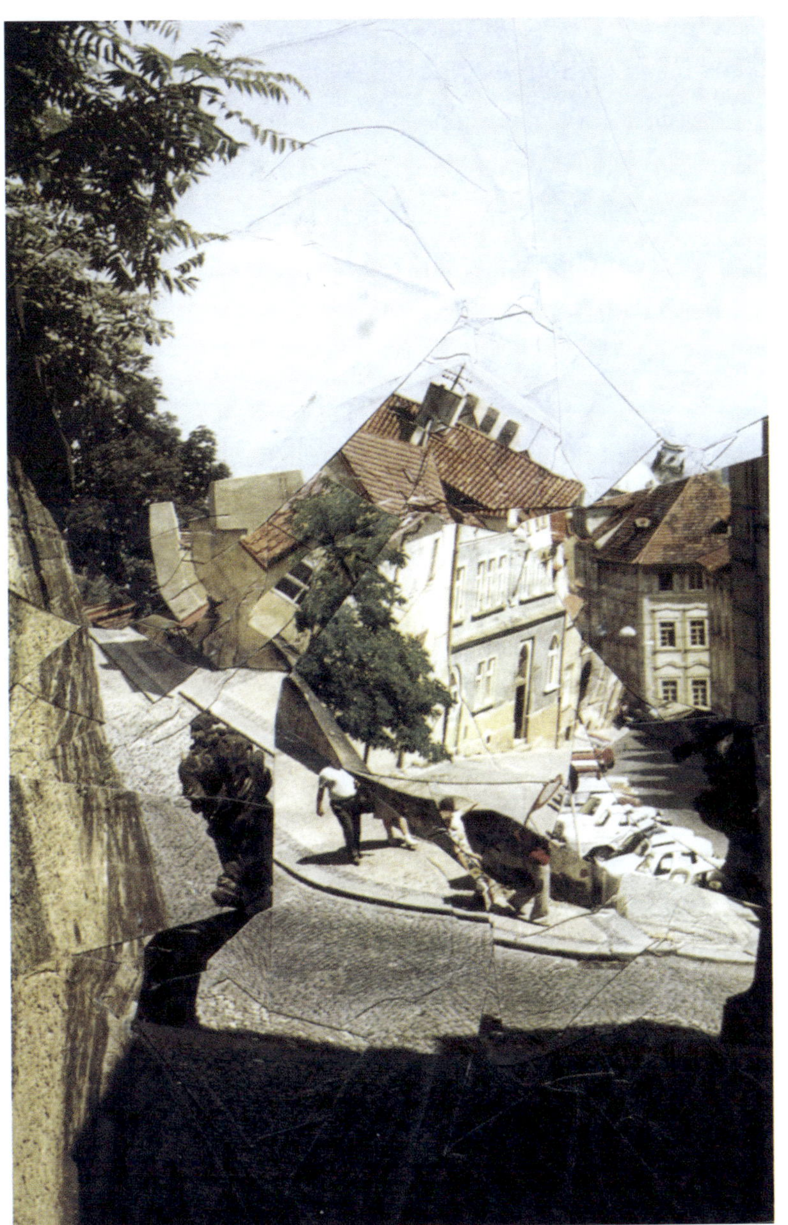

7

... ein irdisches Gebäude ..., aber mit höheren Zielen als das niedrige Häusergemenge und mit klarerem Ausdruck als ihn der trübe Werktag hat.

Das Schloß

... an earthly building ..., but with higher aspirations than the low mass of houses and with a clearer expression than the dull workday.

The Castle

Sala Terrena of the Wallenstein Garden ☞

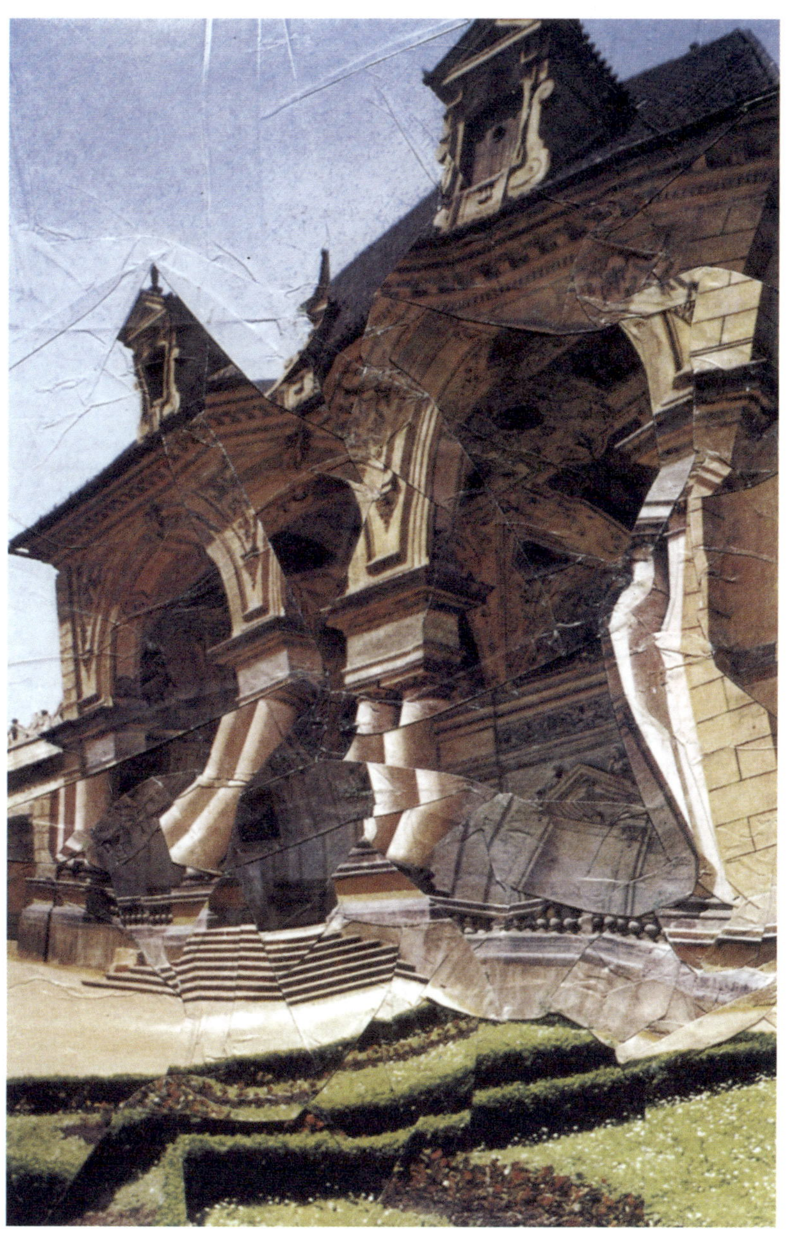

8

Ich habe mich verirrt . . .

Amerika

I have become lost . . .

Amerika

Thunovská Street ☞

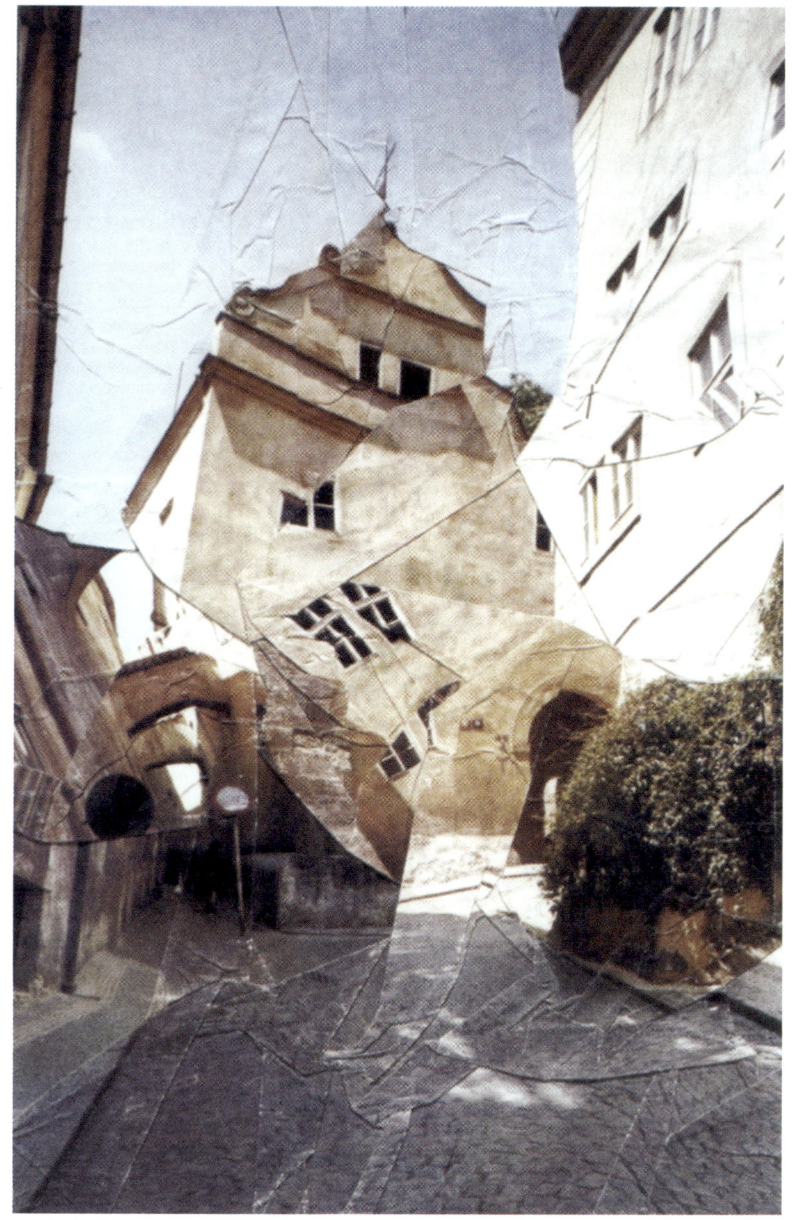

9

Mein Todeskahn verfehlte die Fahrt . . .

»Der Jäger Gracchus«

My death barge went astray . . .

"The Hunter Gracchus"

Grand Priory Mill on Devil's Stream [Čertovka] ☞

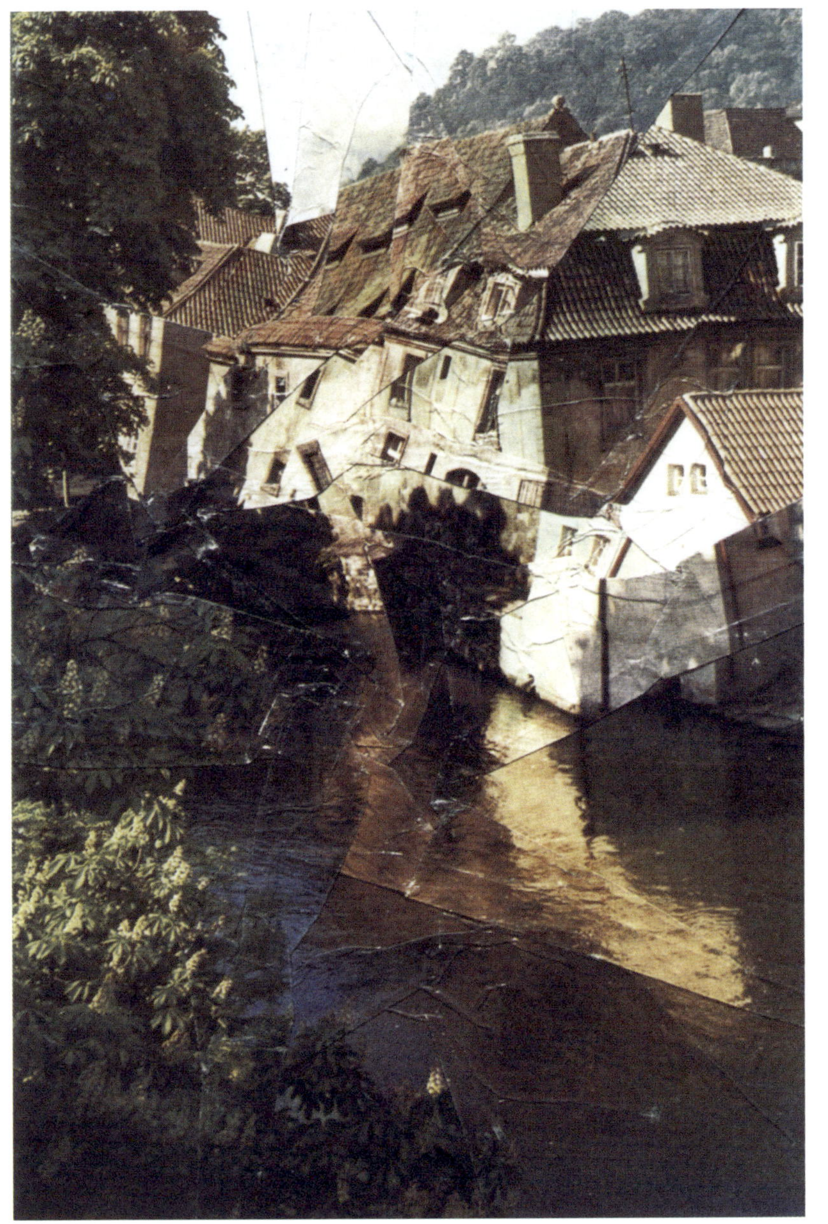

10

Das ist ein Leben zwischen Kulissen. Es ist hell, das ist ein Morgen im Freien, dann wird es gleich dunkel und es ist schon Abend.

Nachgelassene Schriften und Fragmente

It is a life between two scenes. It is bright, it is a morning outdoors, then immediately it becomes dark and it is evening already.

Posthumous Writings and Fragments

House of the White Lion, known as "At the Minute" ☞

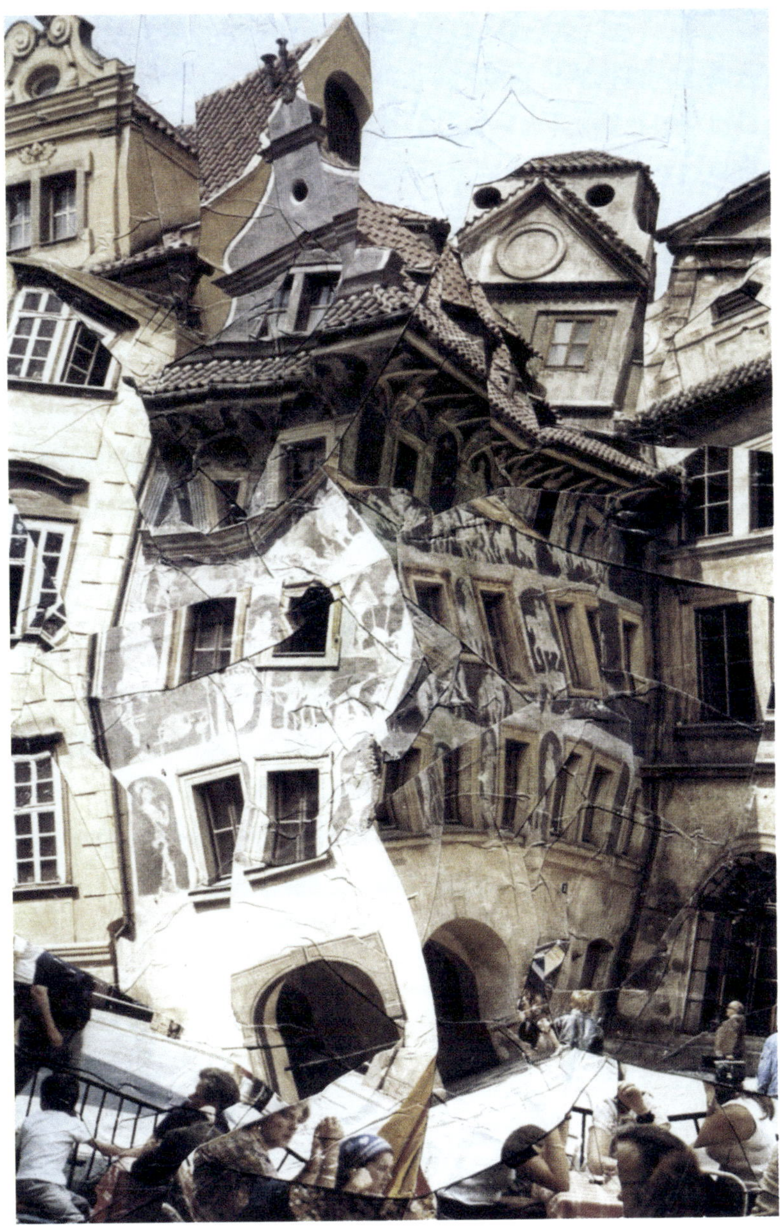

Kafka's home from 1889–96 and where his three sisters were born.

11

Als ich heute meine Treppe hinunterstieg, um vor der Abendgesellschaft noch einen kleinen Spaziergang zu machen, mußte ich mich wundern, wie meine Hände in den Manschetten hin und her schlenkerten, und so lustig haben sie das gemacht. Da dachte ich mir gleich: »Wart, heut kommt was.« Und es ist auch gekommen.

»Beschreibung eines Kampfes«

When I descended my stairs today to take a short walk before the soirée, I was astonished at how my hands swung back and forth in my cuffs, and did this so comically. Then I thought to myself: "Wait, something will happen today." And it did happen.

"Description of a Struggle"

Kolowrat Palace on Valdštejnská Street ☞

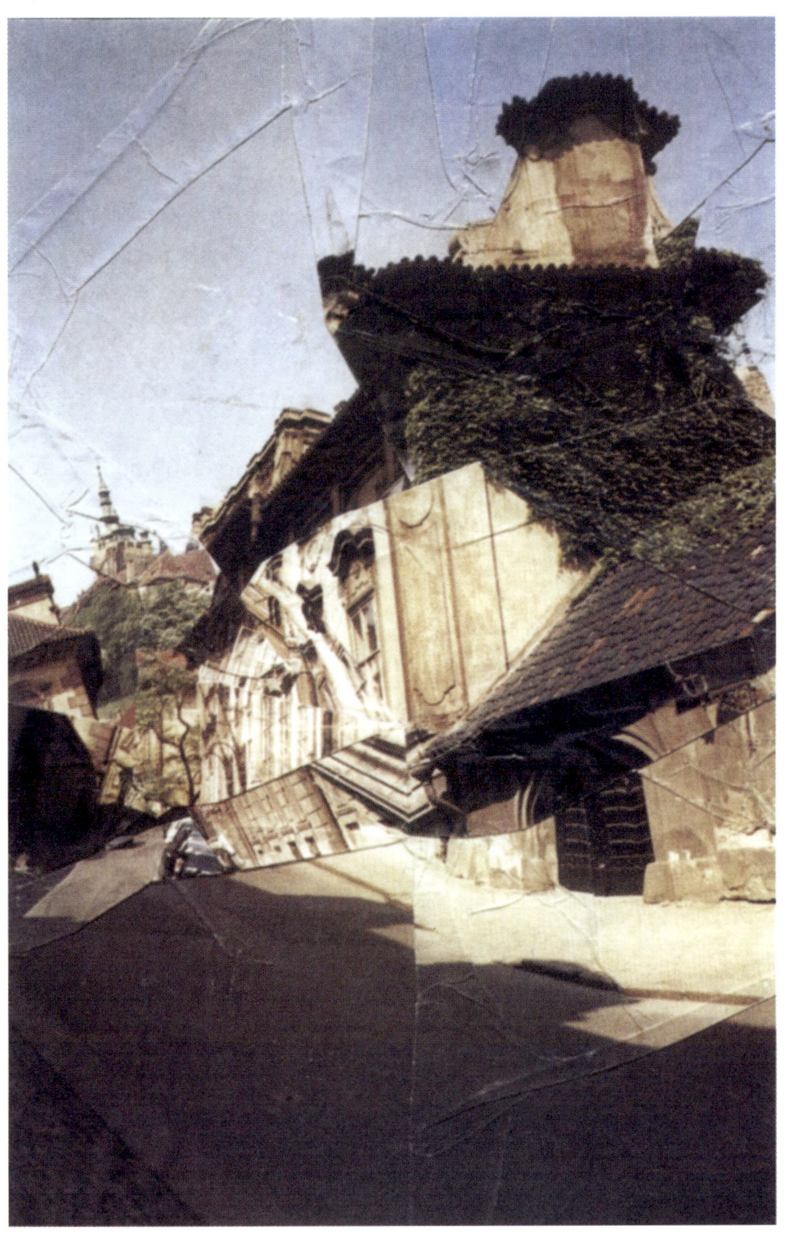

12

In Voraussicht des Kommenden . . .

Nachgelassene Schriften und Fragmente

In a premonition of what is to come . . .

Posthumous Writings and Fragments

Singing Fountain in the Royal Garden ☞

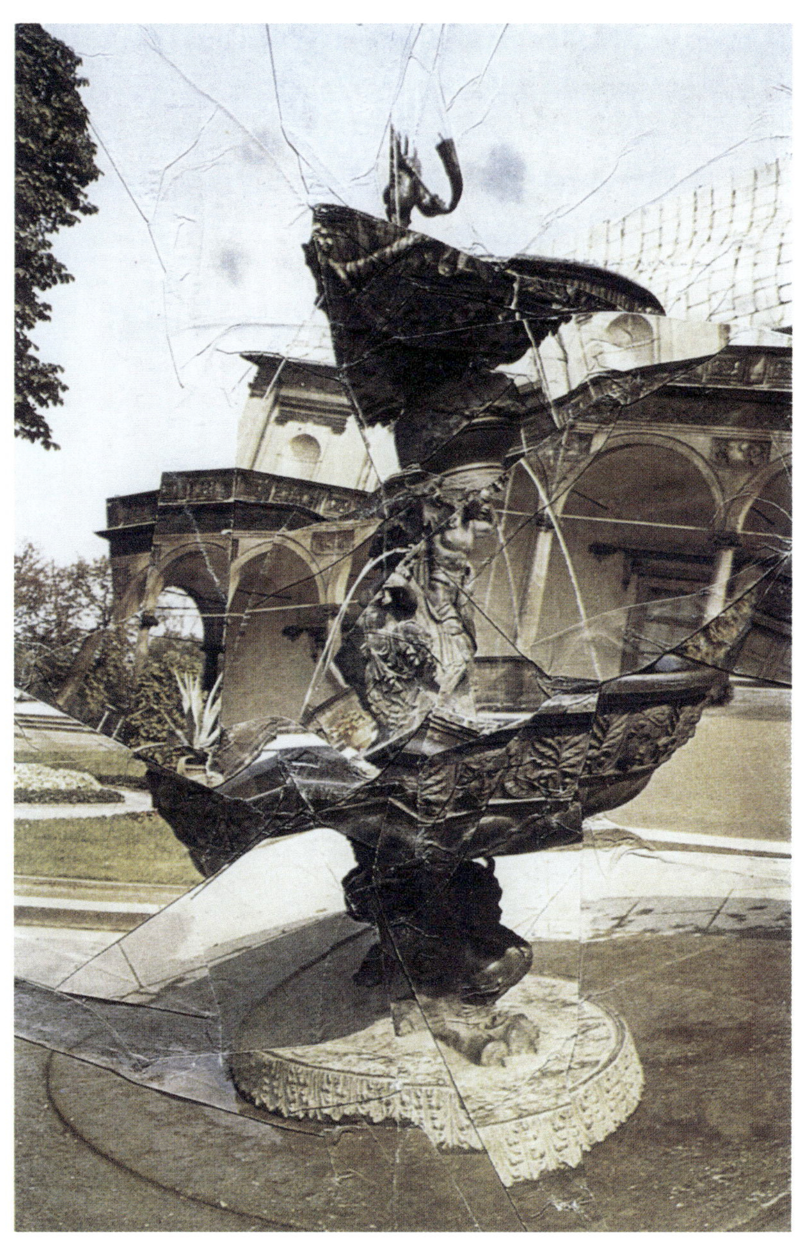

13

War die Welt verkehrt? Wo war ich? Was war denn geschehn?

»Forschungen eines Hundes«

Was the world inverted? Where was I? What had happened?

"Investigations of a Dog"

Golden Lane ☞

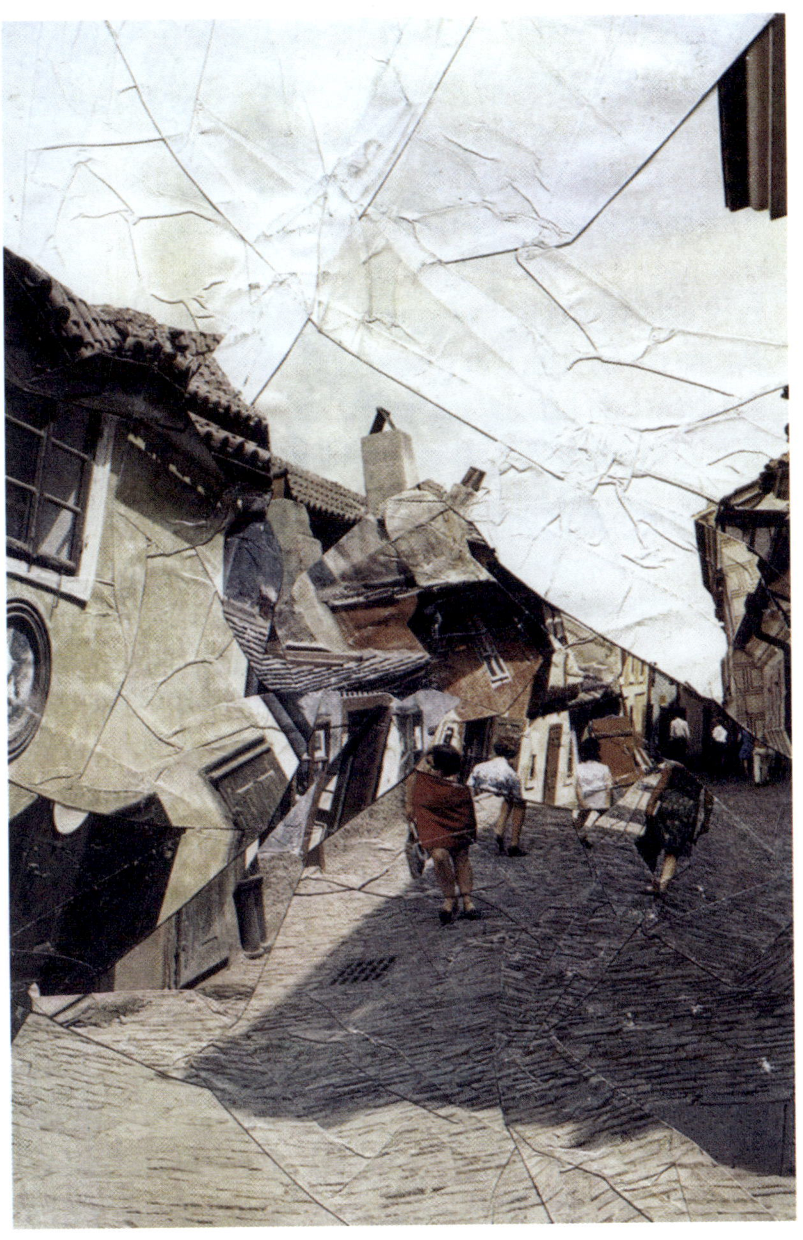

Rented by his sister, Kafka used house No. 22 as a place to write from 1916 to 1917.

14

Es ist nicht so, daß Du im Bergwerk verschüttet bist und die Massen des Gesteins Dich schwachen Einzelnen vor der Welt und ihrem Licht trennen, sondern Du bist draußen und willst zu dem Verschütteten dringen und bist ohnmächtig gegenüber den Steinen, und die Welt und ihr Licht macht Dich noch ohnmächtiger.

Nachgelassene Schriften und Fragmente

It is not that you are buried in a mine and the masses of stone separate you, a weak individual, from the world and its light, but instead you are outside and want to penetrate to the person who has been buried and are powerless against the stones, and the world and its light make you even more powerless.

Posthumous Writings and Fragments

House of the Golden Swan ☞

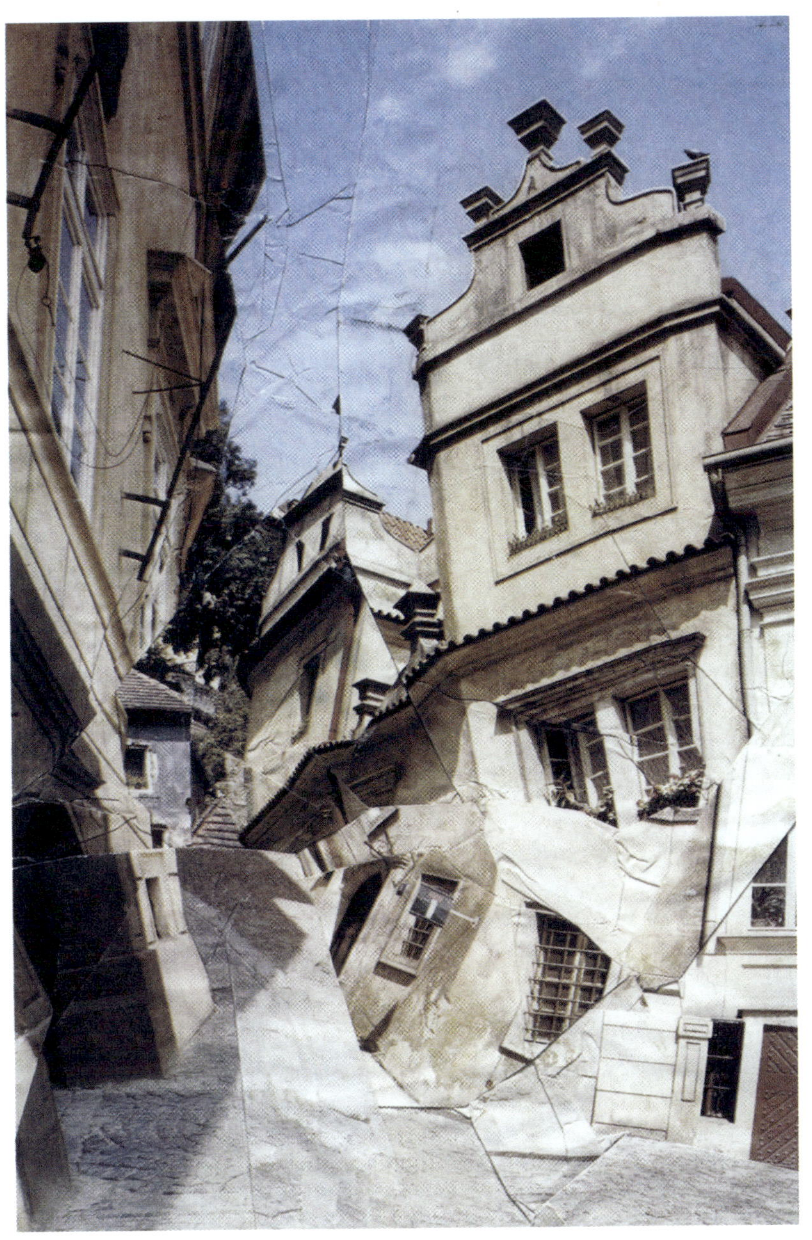

15

Das ist die Rache des Wassers und des Windes; . . .

»Beschreibung eines Kampfes«

That is the revenge of the water and the wind; . . .

"Description of a Struggle"

National Theater ☞

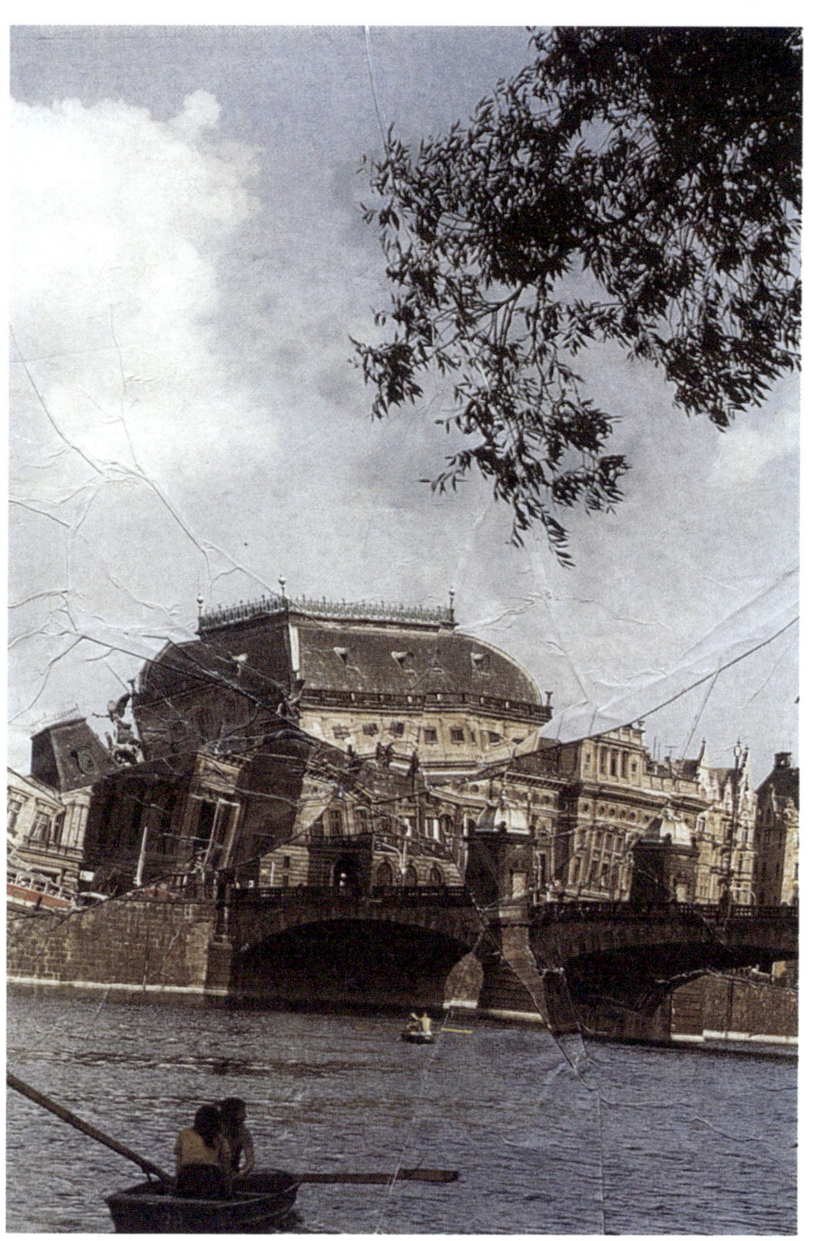

16

Alles fühlt den Griff am Hals.

Nachgelassene Schriften und Fragmente

Everything feels the grip on the throat.

Posthumous Writings and Fragments

Summer Villa Amerika on Ke Karlovu Street ☞

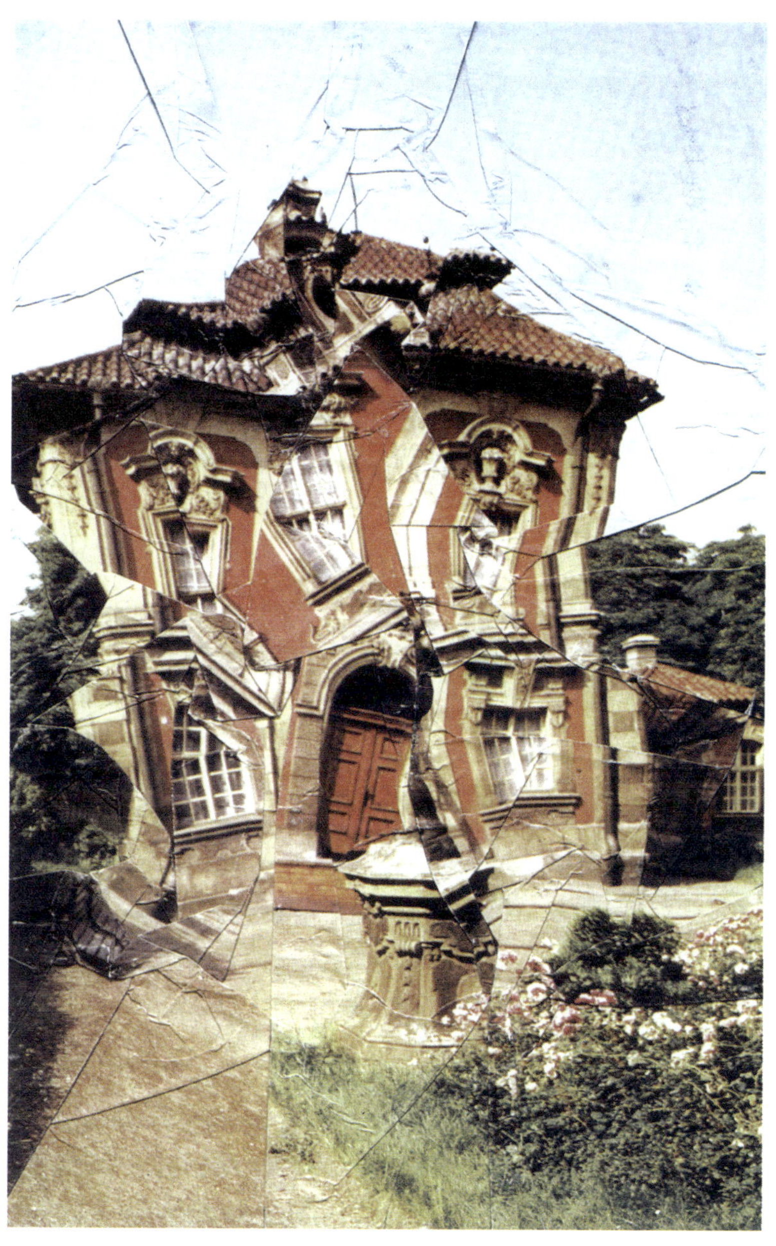

17

. . . solange Du nicht zu steigen aufhörst, hören die Stufen nicht auf, unter Deinen steigenden Füßen, wachsen sie aufwärts.

»Fürsprecher«

. . . as long as you do not stop climbing, the steps will not stop, they will grow upwards under your climbing feet.

"Advocates"

Terrace in the Kolowrat Garden ☞

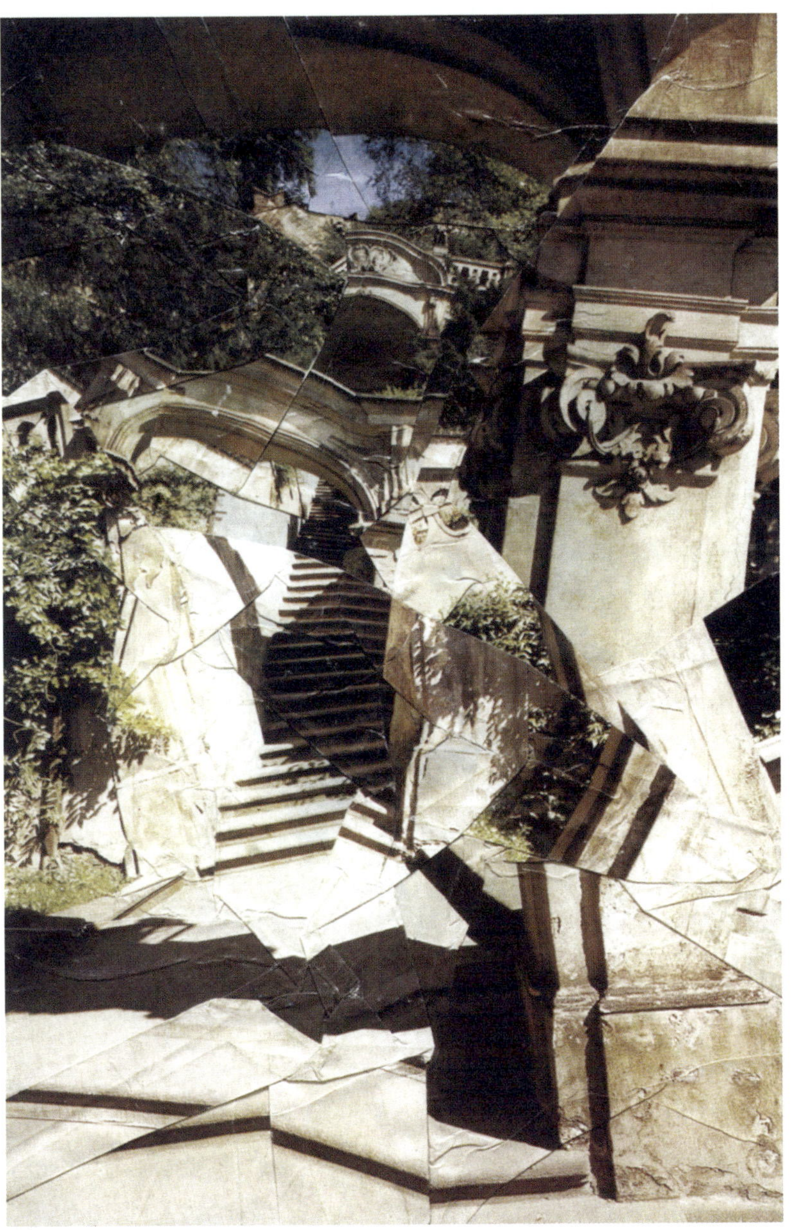

18

Mir ist . . . , als stehe ich nicht vor meinem Haus, sondern vor mir selbst, während ich schlafe, und hätte das Glück gleichzeitig tief zu schlafen und dabei mich scharf bewachen zu können.

»Der Bau«

I feel . . . as though I am not standing in front of my house, but in front of myself while I sleep and simultaneously have the happiness of sleeping deeply and being able to watch over myself closely.

"The Burrow"

House at the Golden Well ☞

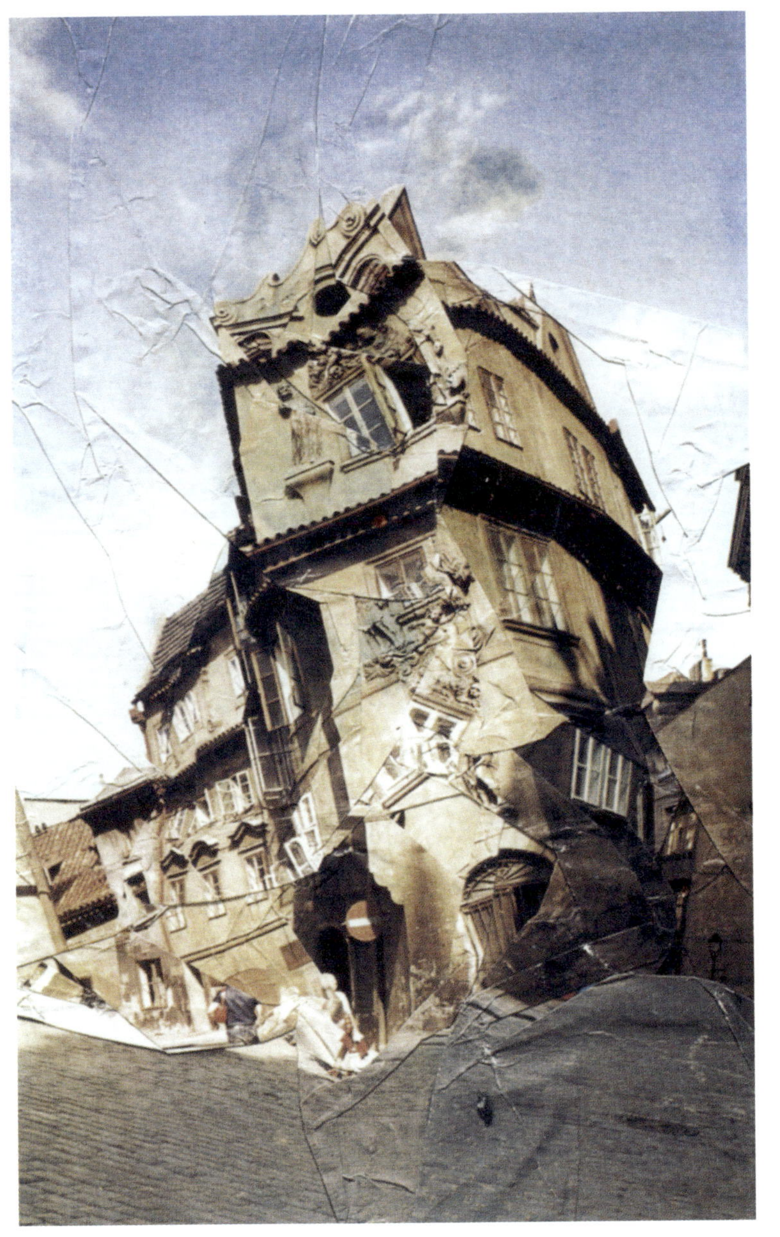

19

Alles ist Phantasie, . . . alles Phantasie, fernere oder nähere . . .

Tagebücher

Everything is fantasy, . . . everything fantasy, further away or closer . . .

The Diaries

Sala Terrena of the Ledeburg Garden ☞

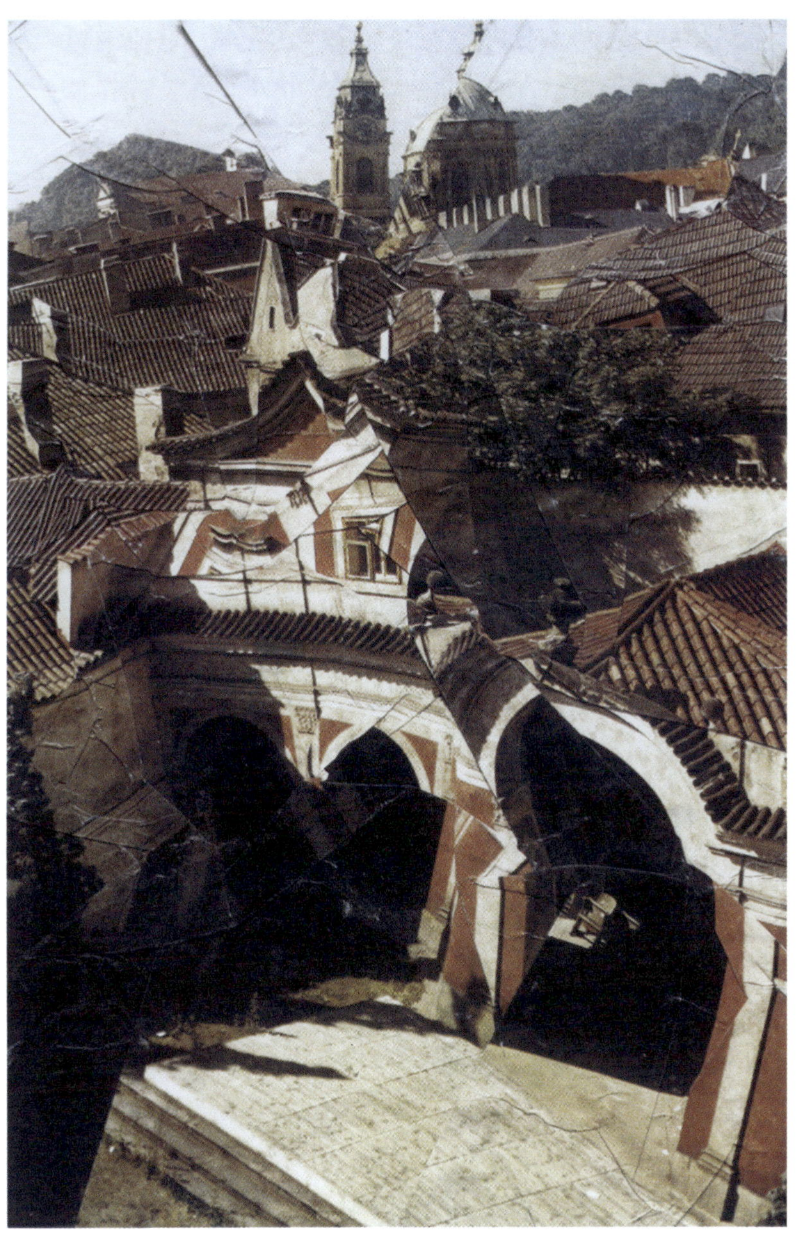

20

Ich war noch nicht umgedreht, da stürzte ich schon, ich stürzte, und schon war ich zerrissen und aufgespießt von den zugespitzten Kieseln, die mich immer so friedlich aus dem rasenden Wasser angestarrt hatten.

»Die Brücke«

I had not yet turned around, then I collapsed, I collapsed and already I was torn and skewered by the sharpened flints that had always stared up at me so peacefully from the raging water.

"The Bridge"

Old Town Bridge Tower ☞

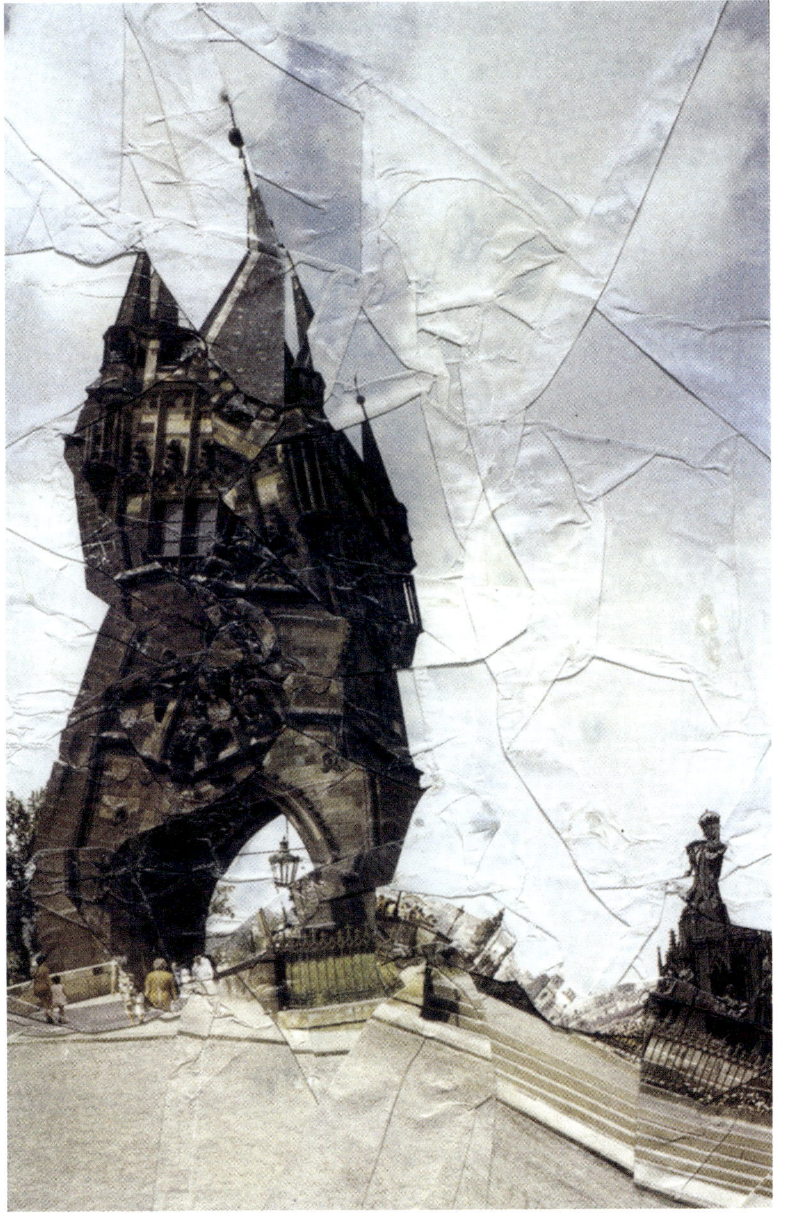

21

Eher ließe sich denken, daß die nächste Generation mit ihrem vervollkommneten Wissen die Arbeit der vorigen Generation schlecht finden und das Gebaute niederreißen werde, um von neuem anzufangen.

»Das Stadtwappen«

It seemed more likely that the next generation with its perfected knowledge would find the work of the previous generation poor and would tear down what had been built to start anew.

"The City Coat of Arms"

St. Nicholas Church, Lesser Town [Malá Strana] ☞

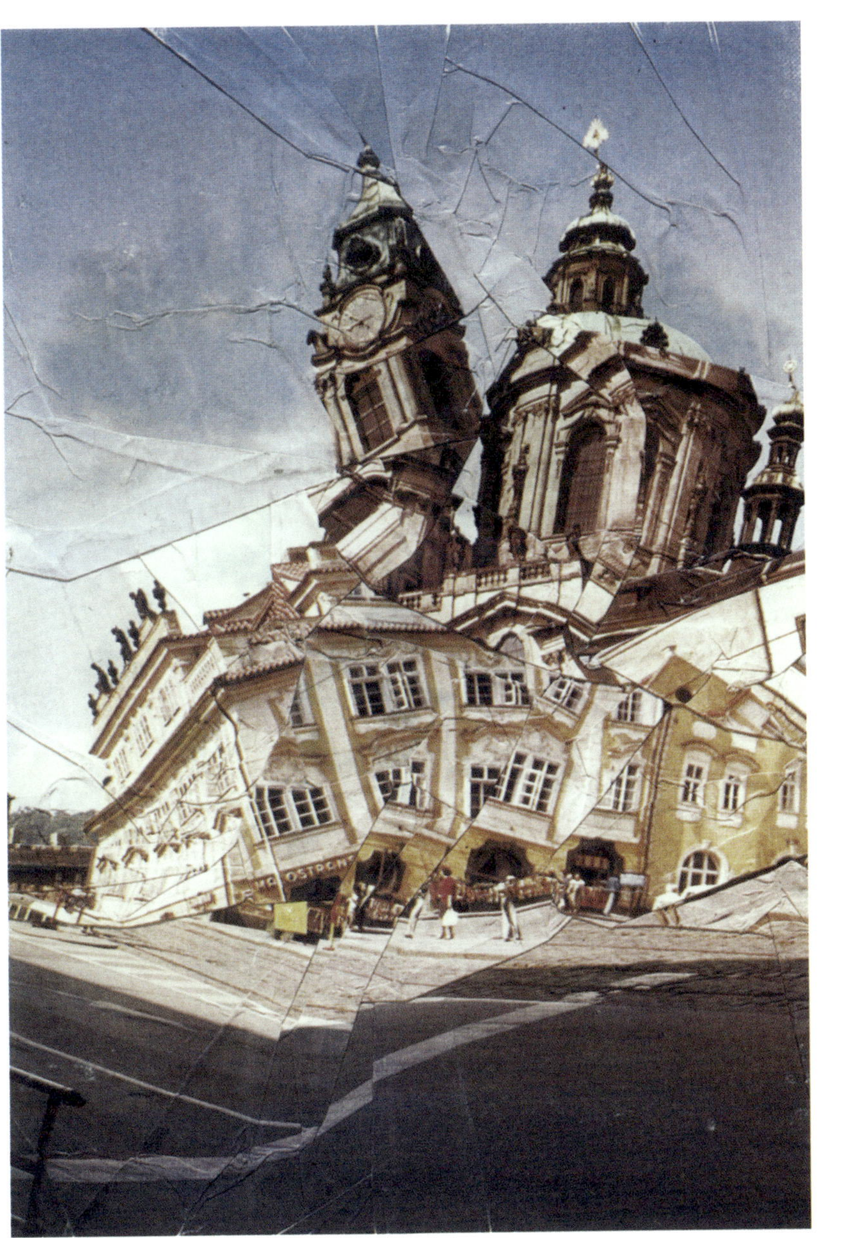

22

. . . das ist ja nichts anderes als Träume . . .

Das Schloß

. . . it is nothing other than dreams . . .

The Castle

Former Hradčany Town Hall ☞

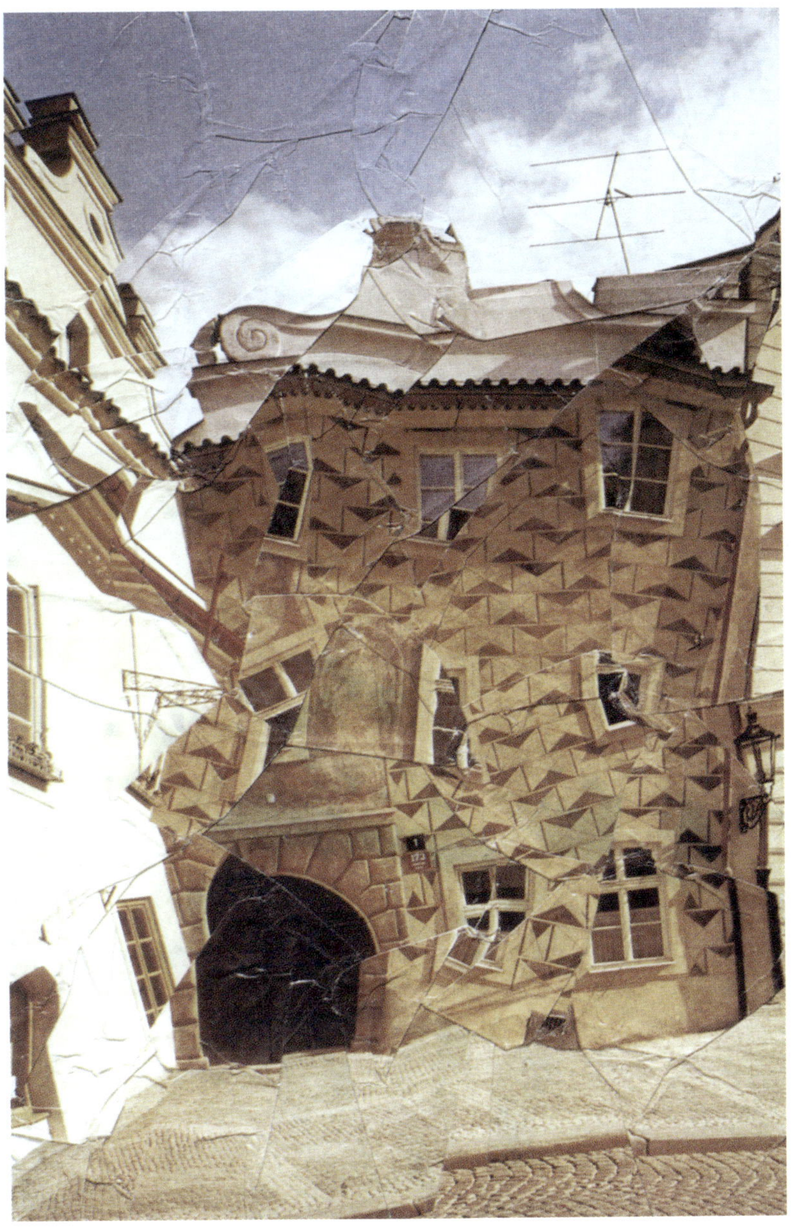

23

»Wie wird es werden?« fragen wir uns alle. »Wie lange werden wir diese Last und Qual ertragen?«

»Ein altes Blatt«

"How will it be?" all of us ask. "How long will we tolerate this burden and torment?"

"An Old Manuscript"

The Loreta ☞

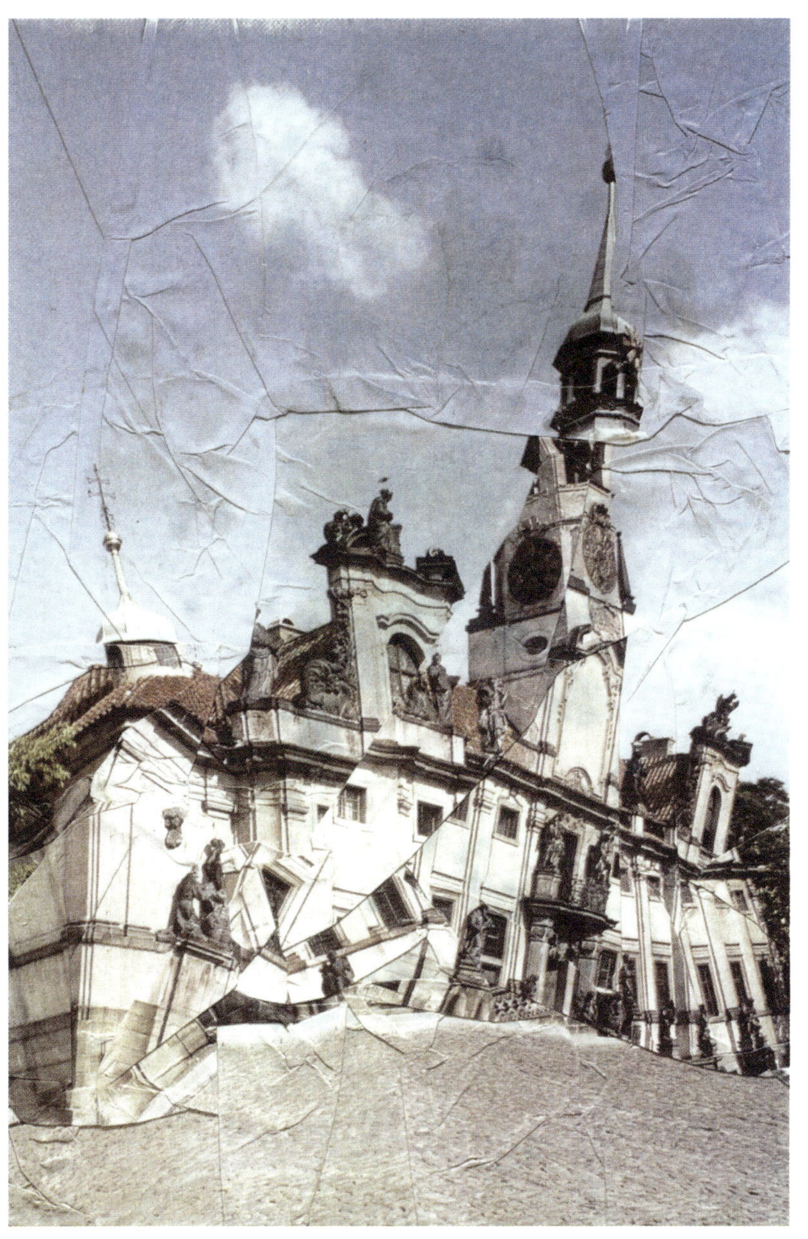

24

Was sind das für Tage, die ich verbringe! Warum ist alles so schlecht gebaut, daß bisweilen hohe Häuser einstürzen, ohne daß man einen äußeren Grund finden könnte.

»Beschreibung eines Kampfes«

What days I spend! Why is everything so poorly built so that tall buildings occasionally collapse without any apparent external reason?

"Description of a Struggle"

Husova Street ☞

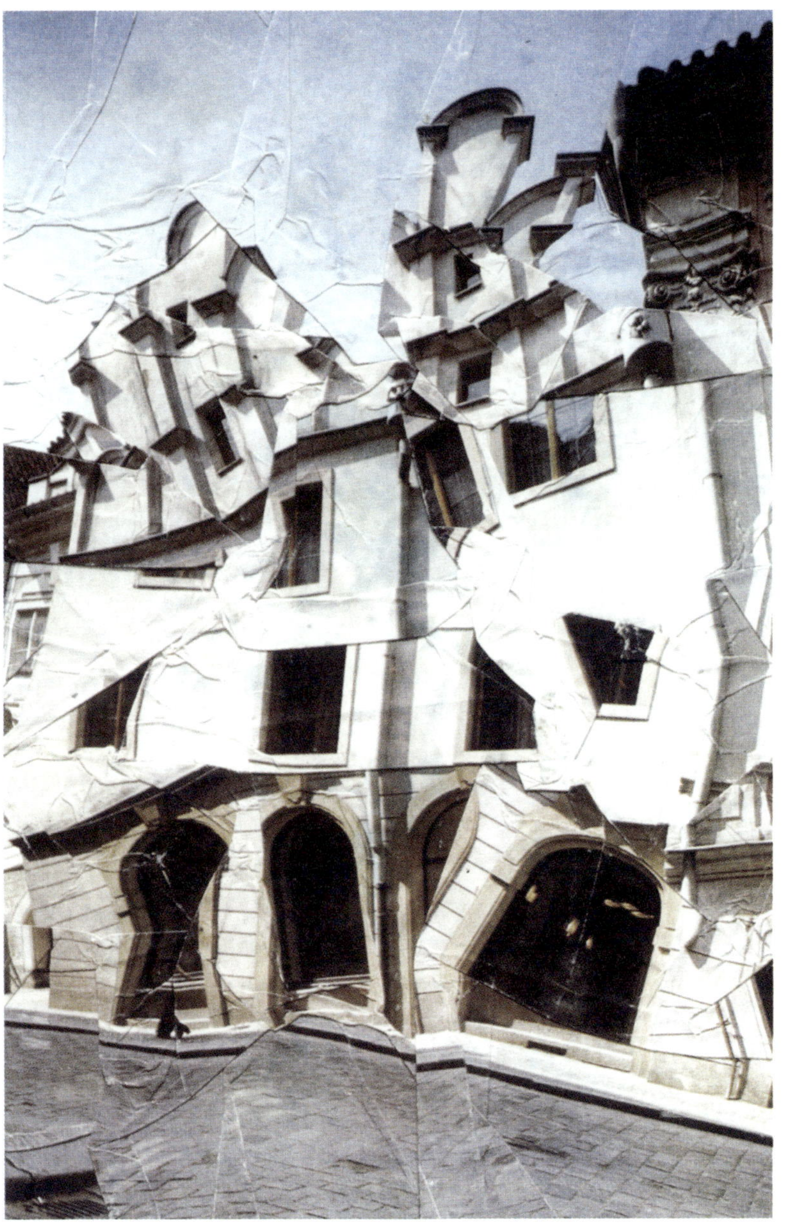

25

»Ach Gott,« sagte er, stand auf, lehnte sich an mich und wir gingen; »da ist ja keine Hilfe . . .«

»Beschreibung eines Kampfes«

"Oh God," he said, stood up, leaned against me, and we walked; "that is no help at all . . ."

"Description of a Struggle"

Old Town Mills with Water Tower ☞

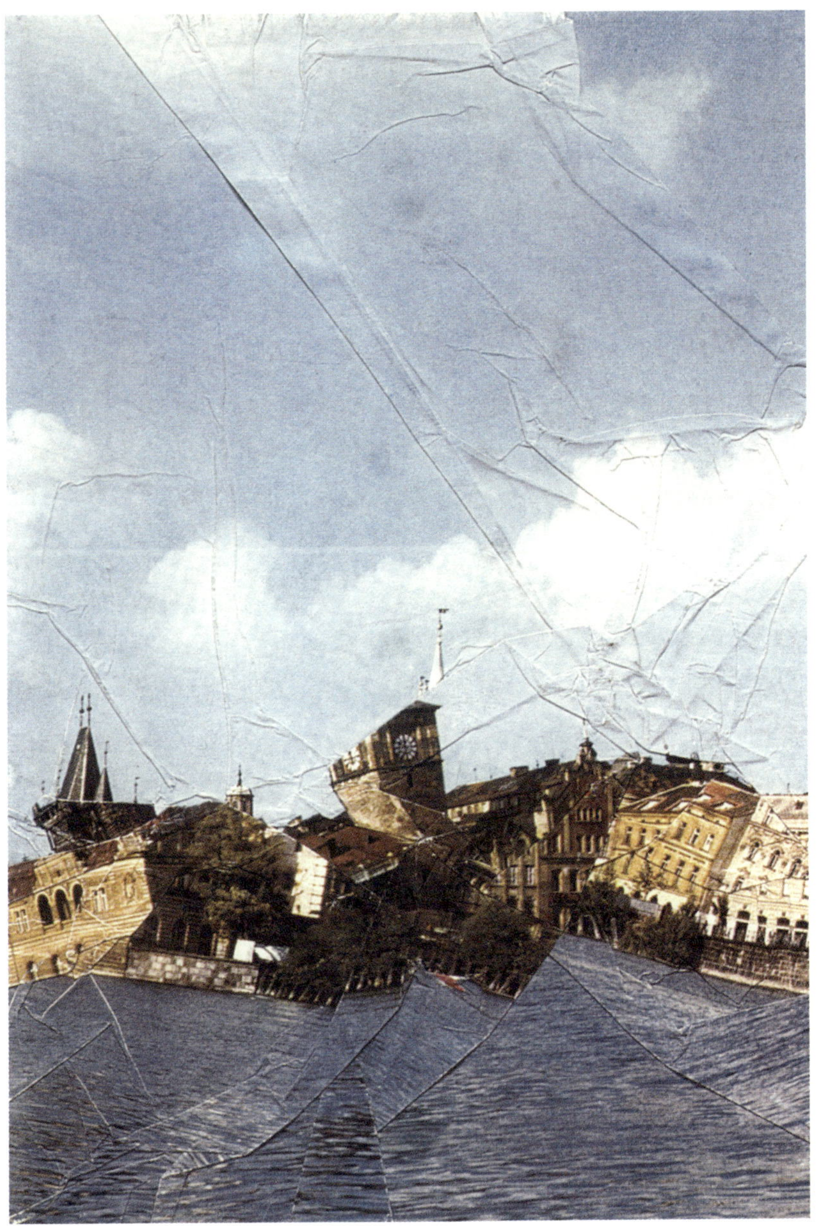

26

Hier ist die Welt, die ich besitze, und ich soll hinüber, einer unheimlichen Zauberei zuliebe, einem Hokuspokus, einem Stein der Weisen, einer Alchymie, einem Wunschring zuliebe. Weg damit, ich fürchte mich schrecklich davor.

Briefe an Milena

Here is the world I possess, and I should go across, for the sake of a sinister magic, a hocus-pocus, a philosopher's stone, an alchemy, for the sake of a ring that grants wishes. Away with it, it completely horrifies me.

Letters to Milena

Prague Castle from the Rudolfinum ☞

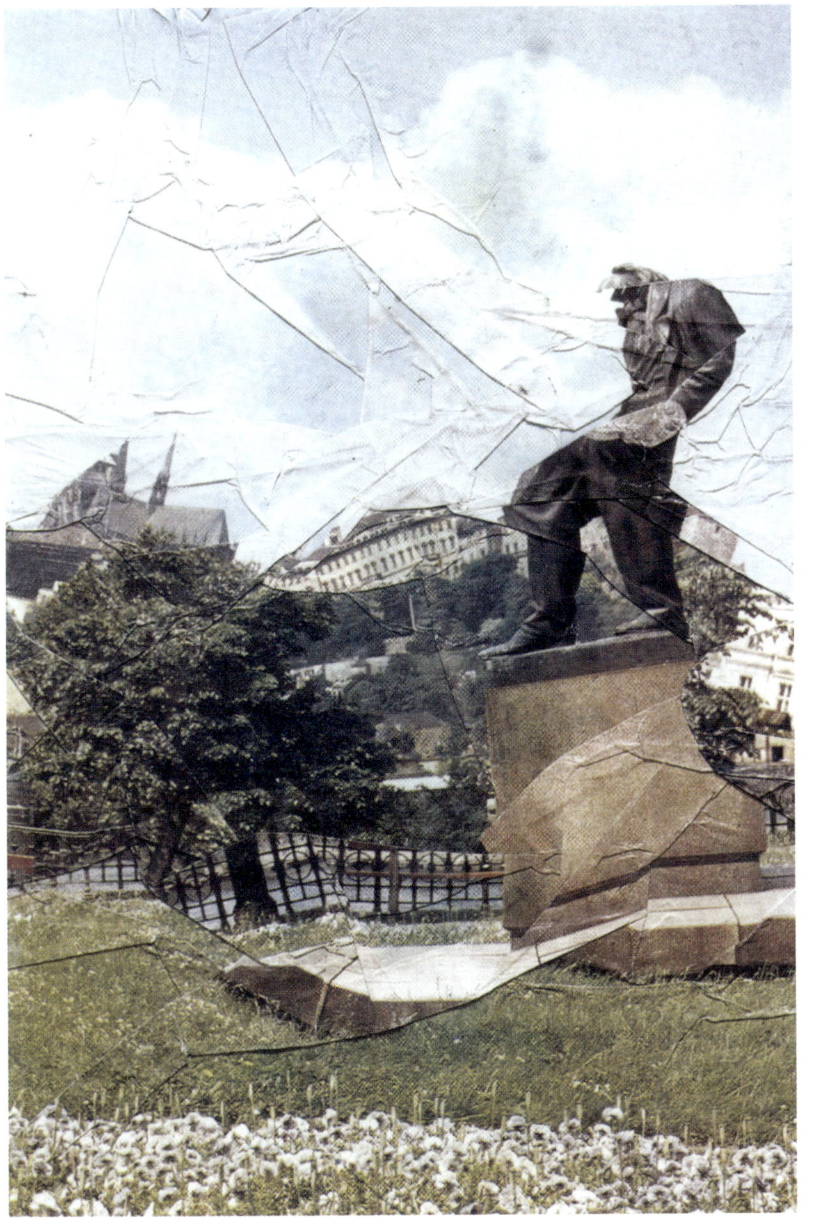

27

Wo dehnt sich die riesige Stadt?

Die Acht Oktavhefte

Where does the colossal city stretch out?

The Eight Octavo Notebooks

Church of St. Laurence on Petřín Hill ☞

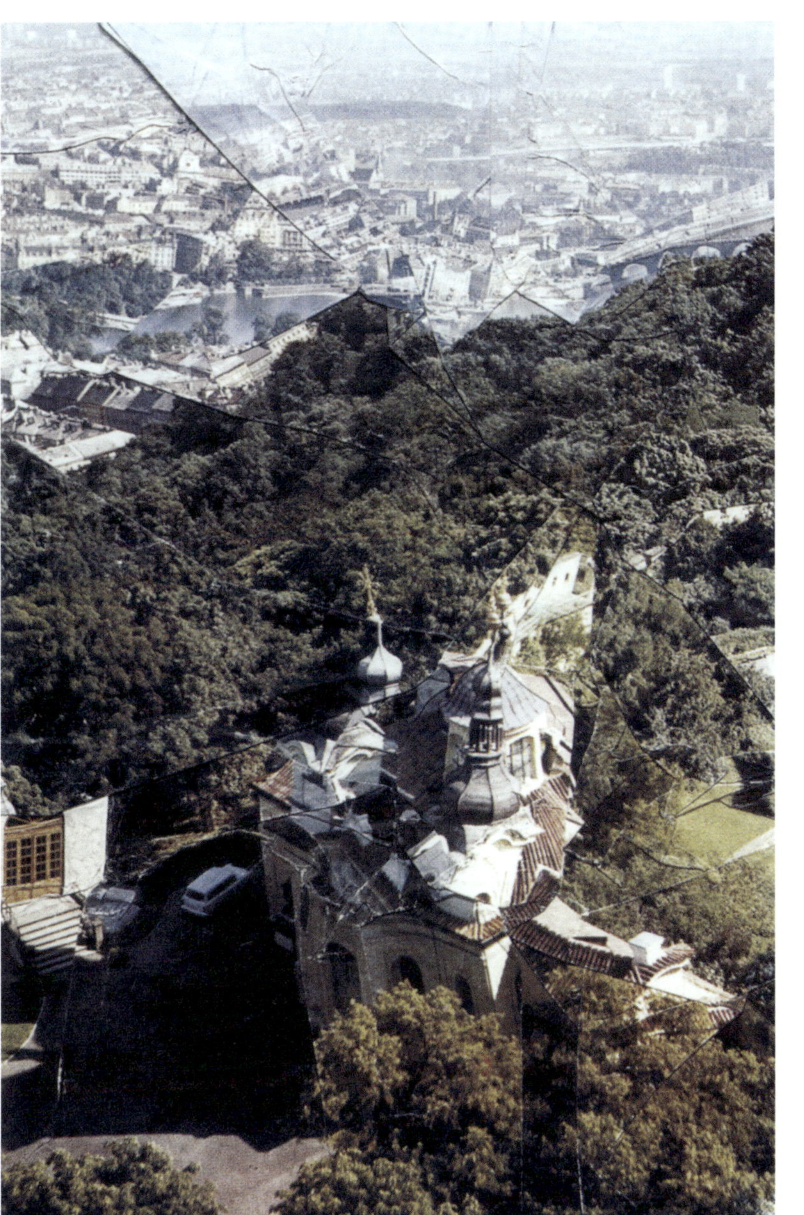

28

»... Dieses Auf und Ab und einige auf diesen Wegen gemachte zufällige, flüchtige, abseitige Beobachtungen sind das Leben.«

Tagebücher

"... Life is this up and down and some fleeting, esoteric observations made at random on these paths."

The Diaries

St. George's Basilica ☞

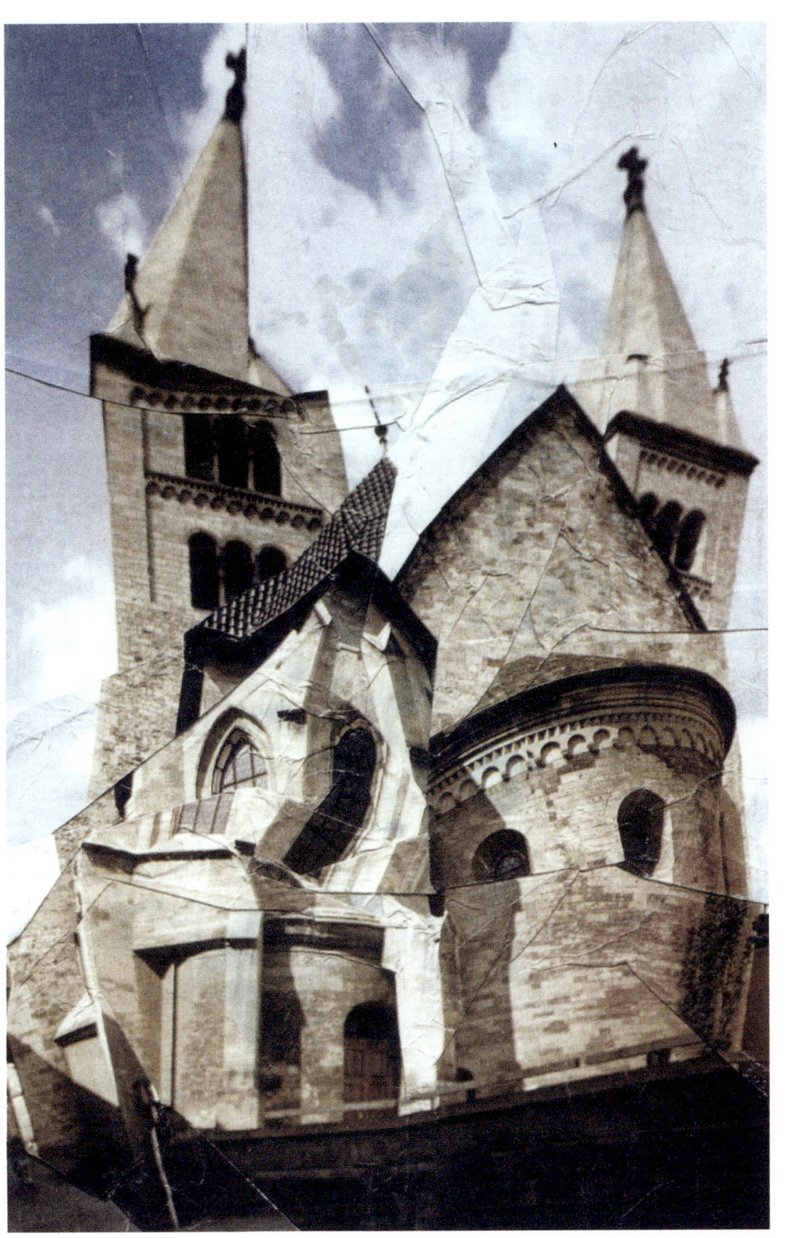

29

Fieber? Wirkliches Fieber? Gemessenes Fieber?

Briefe an Milena

Fever? Real fever? Measured fever?

Letters to Milena

Devil's Stream ☞

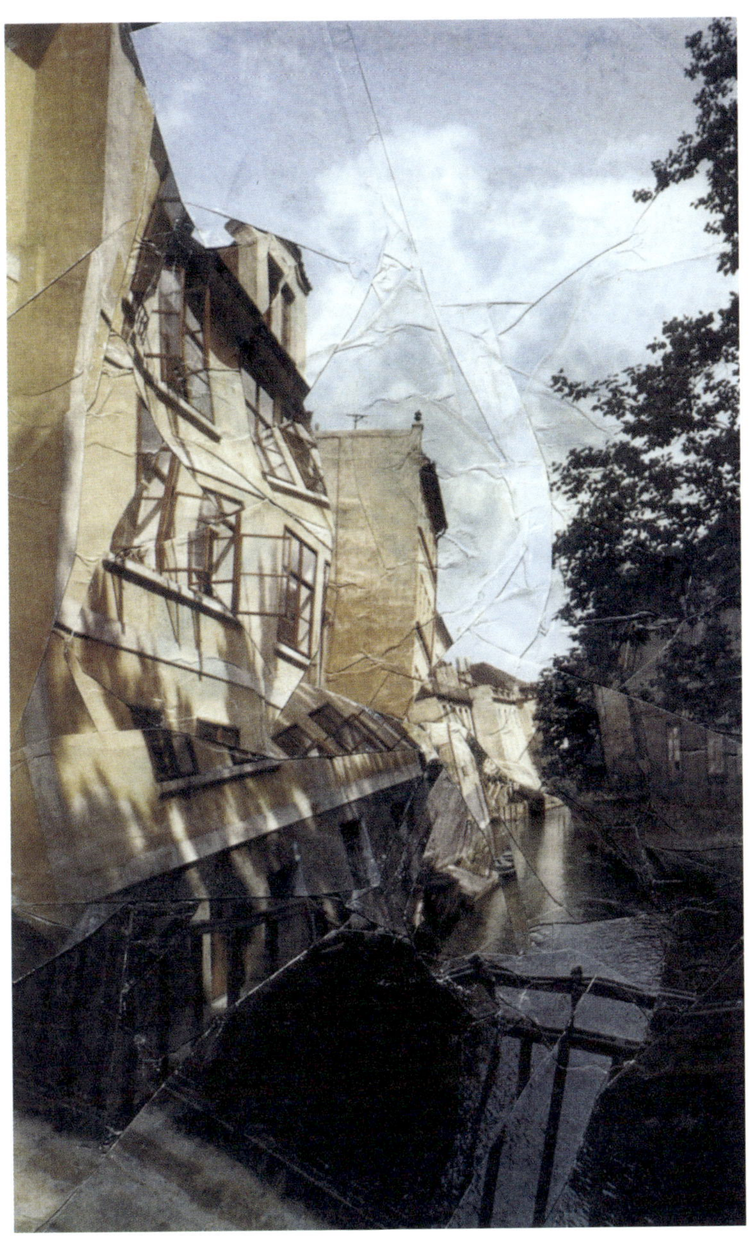

30

Nur unser Zeitbegriff läßt uns das Jüngste Gericht so nennen . . .

Nachgelassene Schriften und Fragmente

Only our concept of time allows us to call it the Last Judgment . . .

Posthumous Writings and Fragments

The Powder Tower ☞

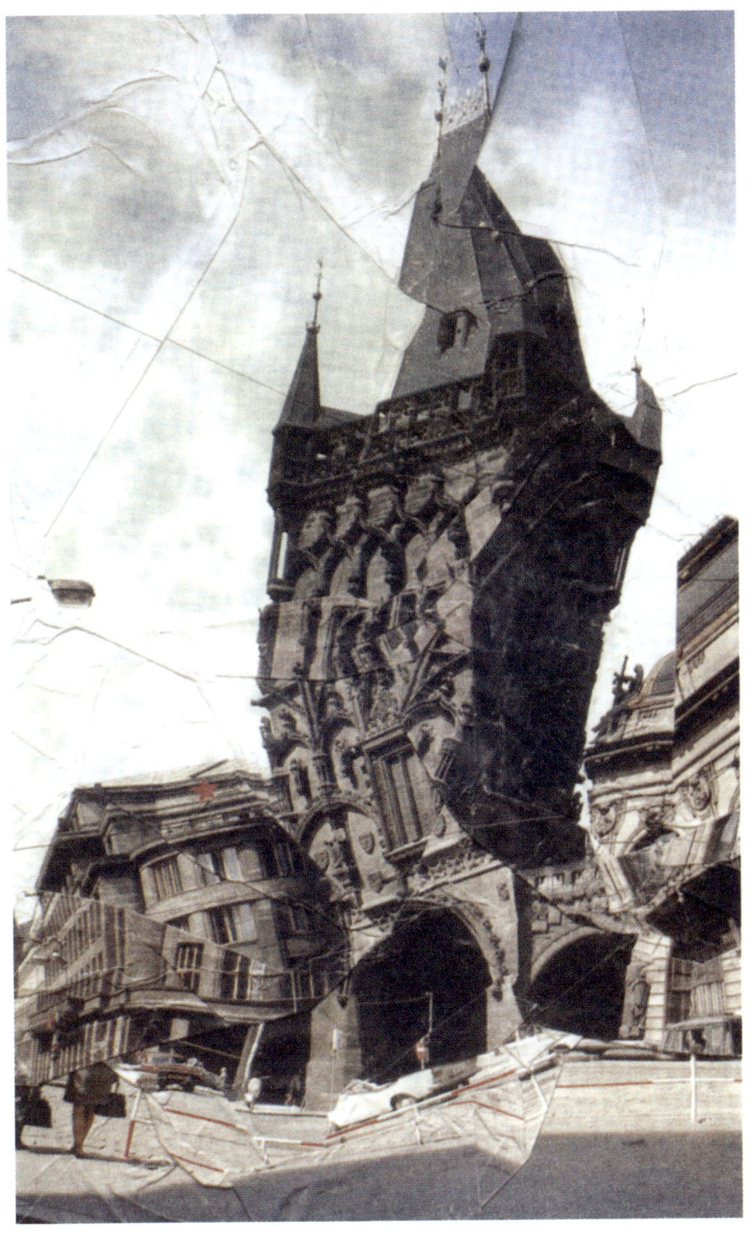

31

»Ein schlimmes Schicksal ... Und Sie tragen gar keine Schuld daran?«

»Der Jäger Gracchus«

"A terrible destiny ... And you bear no responsibility for it?"

"The Hunter Gracchus"

Façade of the Strahov Library ☞

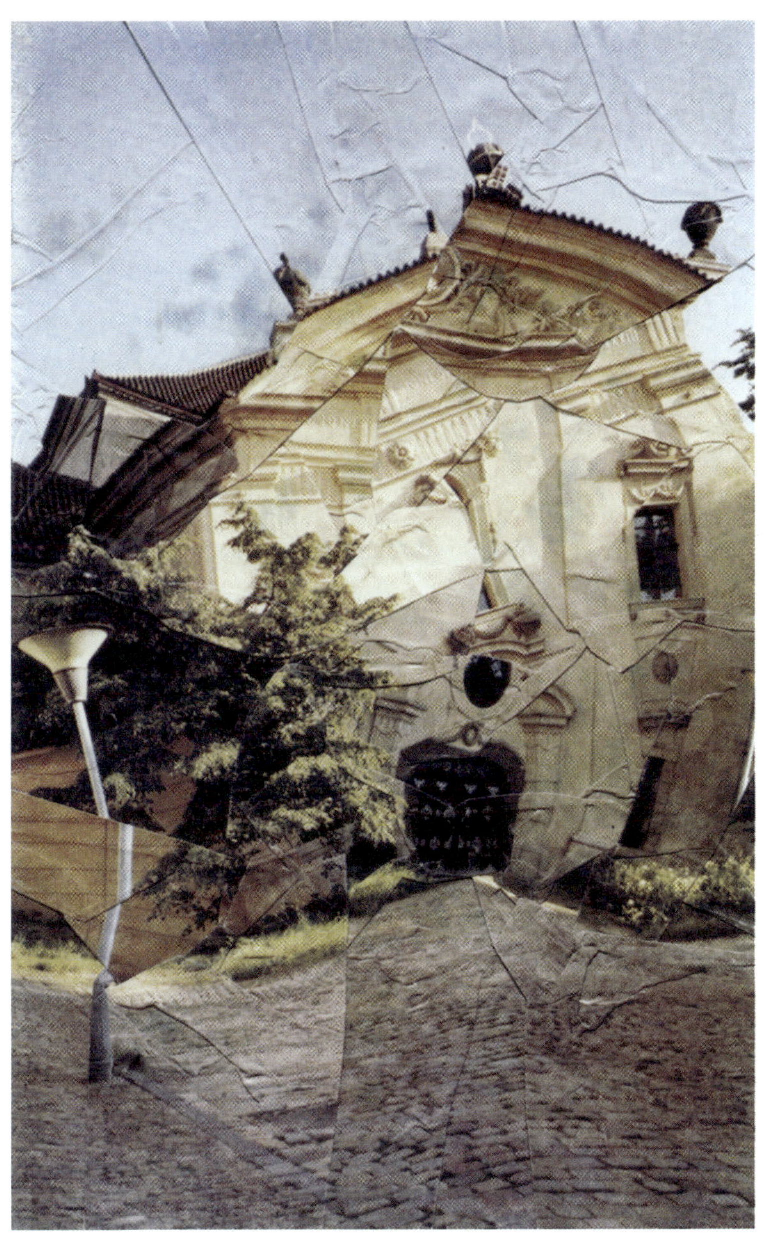

32

Alles was in dieser Stadt an Sagen und Liedern entstanden ist, ist erfüllt von der Sehnsucht nach einem prophezeiten Tag, an welchem die Stadt von einer Riesenfaust in fünf kurz aufeinander der folgenden Schlägen zerschmettert werden wird.

»Das Stadtwappen«

All of the legends and songs that have arisen in this city are fulfilled by the longing for a prophesied day when the city will be smashed by a giant fist with five blows in rapid succession.

"The City Coat of Arms"

Church of Our Lady before Týn ☞

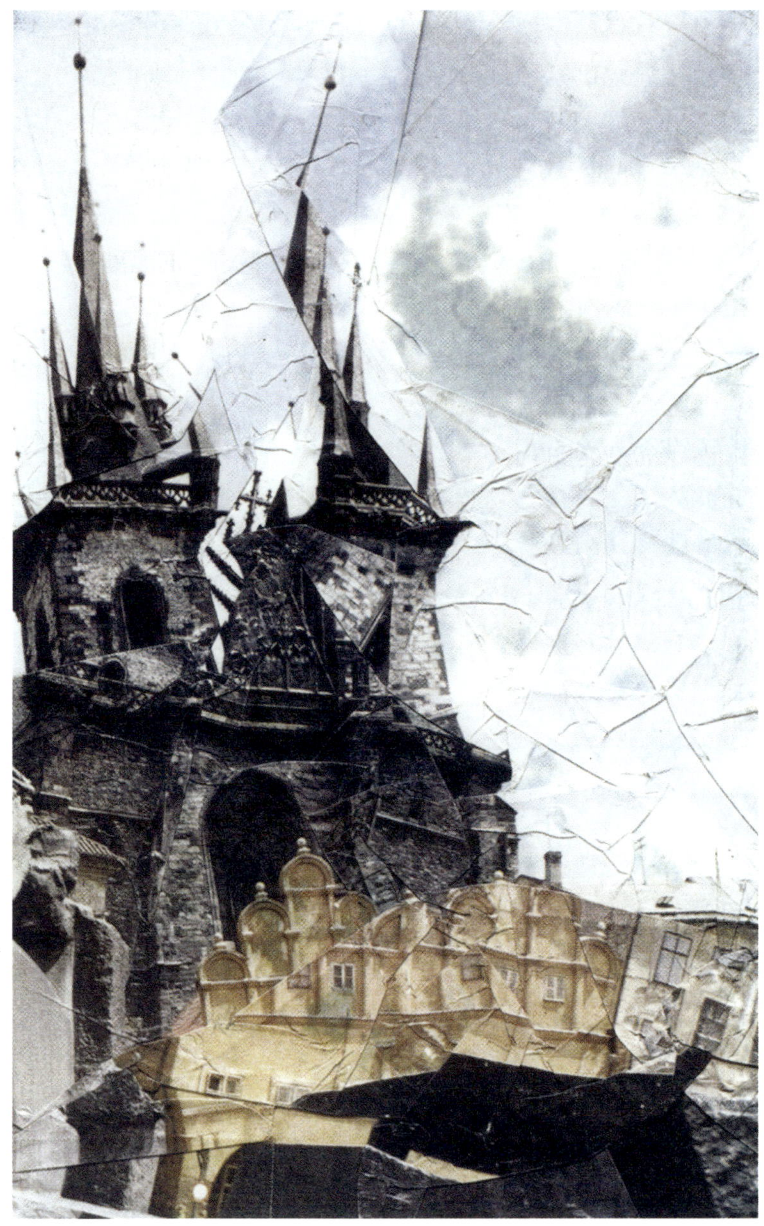

33

Ich mußte weglaufen, es war ganz leicht. Jetzt beim Einbug zur Karlsbrücke nach links konnte ich nach rechts in die Karlsgasse springen.

»Beschreibung eines Kampfes«

I had to run away, it was not easy. Now at the entry to Charles Bridge to the left I could jump into Karlova Street to the right.

"Description of a Struggle"

St. Salvator Church ☞

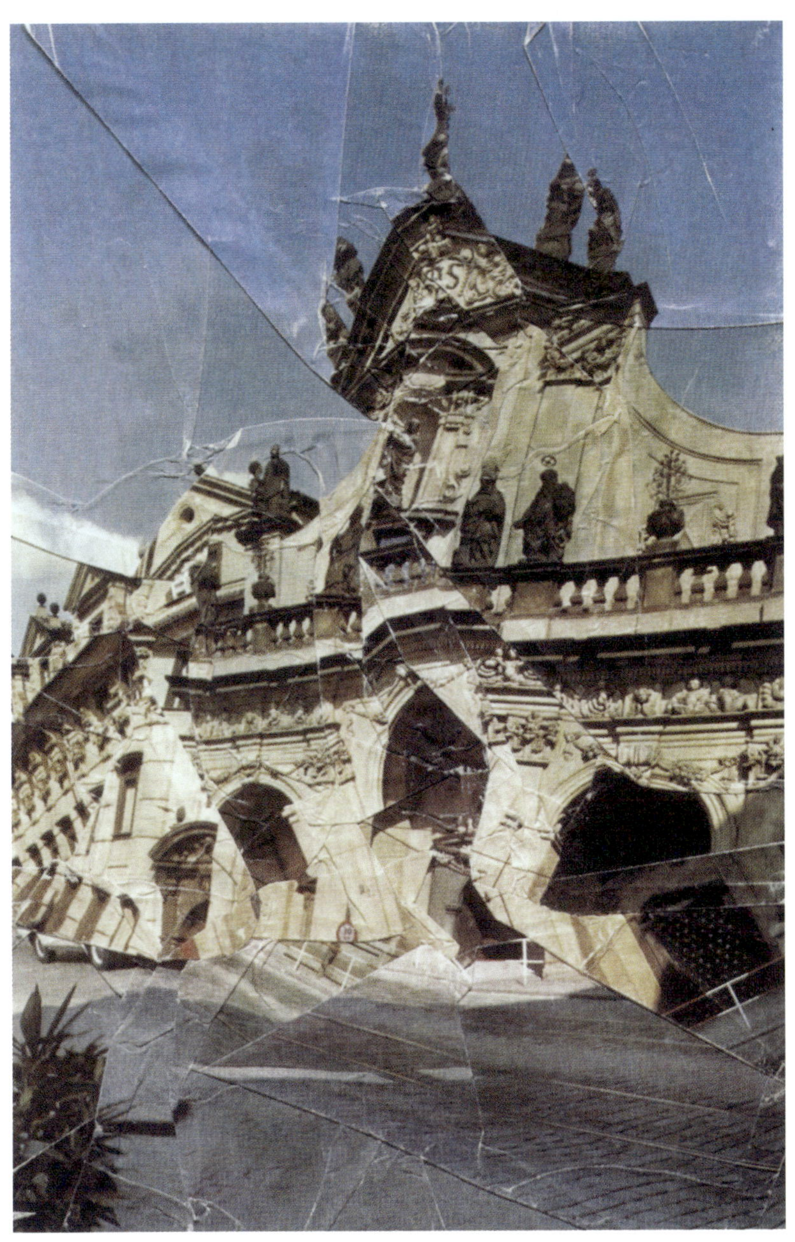

34

Warum wurde ich so lange beschützt, um jetzt so geschreckt zu werden?

»Der Bau«

Why had I been protected for so long to be so terrified now?

“The Burrow”

The Rotunda of St. Martin on Vyšehrad ☞

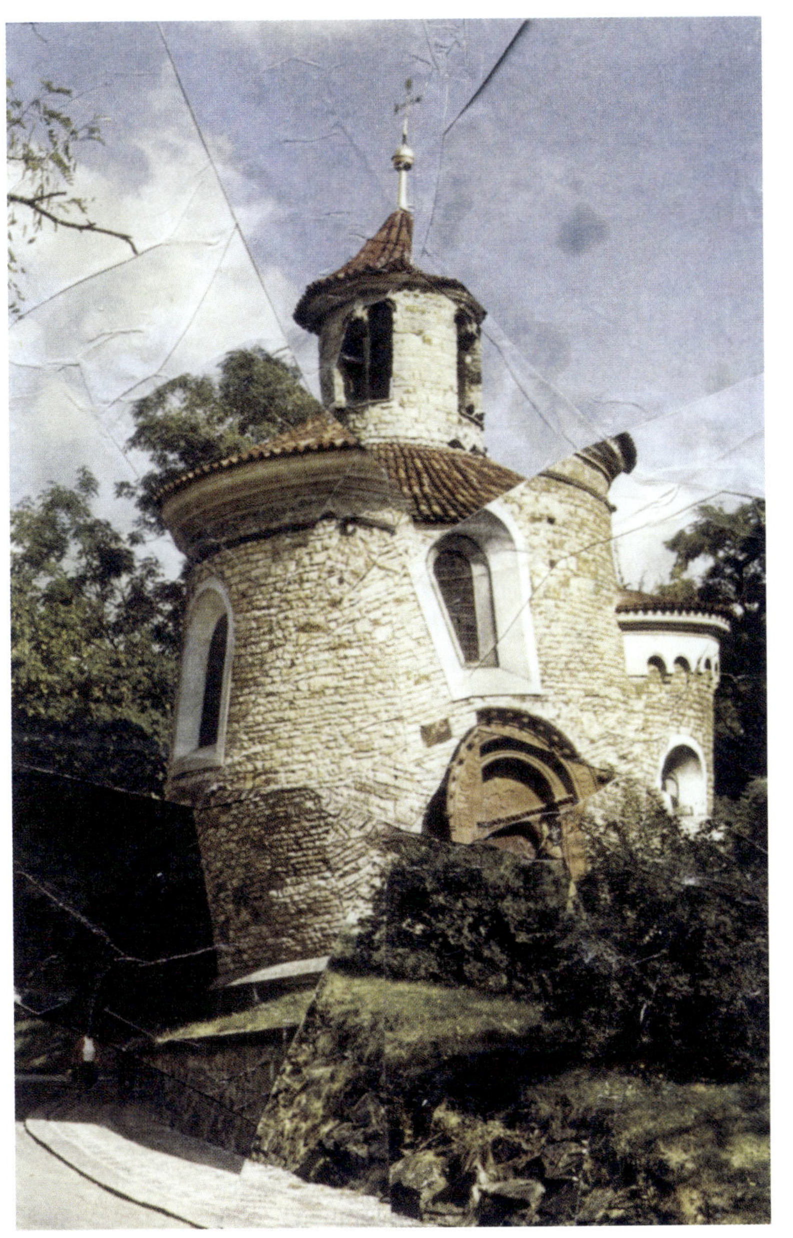

TRANSLATOR'S NOTE

Responses, which Kolář once called "an imaginary interview," was compiled in Prague and Paris in 1973. Though the work offers insights into Kolář's life-long artistic experimentation, it is not simply an artist's statement or manifesto. Comprising seventy-one responses of varying lengths with no questions, the individual texts range across biographical details, descriptions of techniques, and reflections on the artists and writers who influenced him. Despite its fragmentary nature, there is a common thread running through it: Kolář's exploratory approach to art and literature through which he engages with their history, major works, and the very materials of writing and painting to seek new avenues of expression.

"So nothing completely new can ever really be invented," he writes in the first response in reference to art and science, fields that for him shared a common investigative nature. Though this statement might seem peculiar at first for an artist who was defined by inventiveness, it is not necessarily incompatible with his techniques if viewed as a description of the parameters within which creativity takes place rather than as a proscriptive command. Artistic activity is, according to Kolář, circumscribed by its nature, by the materials and practices that form a framework in which an artist works. In doing so, the work becomes something new, not in the sense of unprecedented, but as something recontextualized or repurposed. As he states in the second response, "As in science, every new discovery in art broadens the field of human perception and understanding." Kolář is not creating anything new per se but new ways of looking at what is already there.

Kolář's initial experiments assumed, relatively speaking, a more traditional literary form. He wrote poetry and prose from the late 1940s through most of the 1950s. His early collections, starting with *Baptismal Certificate* (1941) through to *Days in a Year* (1948), were soon published after completion. Subsequent collections had to wait until the late 1960s and after to see publication since following the Communist takeover in 1948 he was deemed a political undesirable, even landing in prison for nine months in 1953. Despite the appearance of his poems – mostly in samizdat – in the 1960s, Kolář's output was increasingly shaped by a desire to "go beyond verbal expression," as Jindřich Chalupecký once put it. He called this nonlinguistic method "evident poetry." It involved arranging visual elements instead of words in verse. They were among his earliest attempts to draw nonlinguistic elements into poetry while still involving the process of writing, or processes akin to writing.

The "muteness" of his evident poetry, also known as silence poetry, of the 1960s could be interpreted as a reaction to the ideological constraints on expression — they were a way to speak when the language of literature at the time mostly required the official sanction of the Communist regime's Writers' Union. While in private Kolář lamented the "parroting of directives" he witnessed, little of this sentiment is overtly addressed in *Responses*. In fact, the text is mostly reticent about politics. Five years prior to its composition, Soviet tanks rolled into Czechoslovakia, ushering in a period of increased political repression known as normalization. Persecution and censorship intensified, people fled, others were imprisoned on political grounds, and the vast majority of the population adjusted to a life of even more circumscribed possibilities. Yet *Responses*, despite a passing reference to the Nazi occupation, has very little to say, at least directly, about the Communist regime. Nor does it comment much on the work of other Czechoslovak writers and artists. Bohumil Hrabal is referenced twice, Urbánek, Piesen, and Malich just once. Other significant contemporaries with whom he was close, such as Vladimír Boudník or Josef Hiršal or Václav Havel, do not feature at all. The text predominantly revolves around Kolář's artistic practice and influences.

Chalupecký argued that Kolář's shift from conventional writing in the 1960s is best seen in poetic rather than political terms. Kolář wasn't silent because language had become so tainted by officialese as to be irredeemable but rather because language had become exhausted of creative potential. Yet, as *Responses* reveals, his fascination with language persisted: "I had to obtain material on the origins of writing in general." Elsewhere he employs the language of biology: "I also needed to know the composition of a word's blood cells," and physics: "certain clusters of words represent powerful fields of energy." Art and science both are part of his project, the allusions to science revealing a view of language as something material rather than an abstract system of symbols. As such, it interacts with other objects, creating a world comprising these multifaceted interactions, sites of meaning that Kolář explores through art and literature.

Seen in these terms, Kolář's artistic experimentation was not a way out of these interactions. Instead, to belabor the spatial metaphor, it provided a way in, an avenue for interrogating the parameters of the artistic practices in which he worked. As many have noted, his visual art is based on a fragmentation of both word and image, a destruction of their given context to create a new one. To draw a line, however, from his literary influences to his visual work is not a matter of convenient interpretation. Jumping between the two poles of literature and visual art, *Responses* embodies this preoccupation and reveals through its fragmented nature that for Kolář there was no strict distinction between them: "My interest from the beginning has been to locate the points of friction between visual art and literature."

The pairing of *Responses* with the collage series *Kafka's Prague* should be seen in this context. If it is not a culmination of Kolář's reinvention, then it's certainly a testament to it, since his interest in collage dates back to the 1930s when he was first "enthralled" by Surrealism. His early work relied on the juxtaposition of unaltered images, techniques he called rapportage and confrontage. Over time, his techniques evolved, becoming so distinct that each one required the coining of a new term, the number ultimately exceeding 120. The crumplages of *Kafka's Prague* are created from images of famous Prague landmarks as well as houses and streets, places of importance in Kafka's life. Crumplage, a portmanteau word combining "crumple" and "collage" (*muchláž* in Czech), involved the meticulous moistening and crumpling of paper, the results of which are "the brother of chance." The new image that emerged as a result of the creasing became the point of the piece. As Charlotta Kotik once remarked: "Just as words take on different meanings each time they are used within a new syntax, an image also speaks in different ways when placed into a new visual configuration."* That the series was originally conceived as a *leporelo*, which can be a pop-up picture book or a concertina book, underscored Kolář's ongoing preoccupation with the intersection of the literary and the visual.

Interestingly, Kolář's collage techniques highlight the continued role language played in his work because the meaning of his visual

*Charlotta Kotik, *Jiří Kolář: Transformations* (Buffalo: Albright-Knox Art Gallery, 1978), 13.

work is derived, at least in part, from the extensive idiosyncratic nomenclature he invented to classify them. Crumplage, rollage, prollage, Magrittage, and chiasmage, to name just a few of his lexical creations, dictate how the viewer should understand the visual work and appreciate it as something singular. The names of these techniques bring to mind Kolář's notion of a word being part of a field, in this case one that includes his collages. For this reason, a translation has to respect not only the meaning but the effect of a word. Many of the terms have been translated to preserve a reference to the underlying principle of each technique, which Kolář perceived as a discrete practice.

As an "imaginary interview," the translation has also tried to preserve the text's conversational tone as well as its occasional wooden phrases and syntax, as if mimicking Communist apparatchik-speak. It should not be read as a transcript, but rather as a creation in its own right where the flow and juxtaposition of ideas imitates the associative spontaneity of speech, which he viewed as distinct from poetic language. For Kolář, it was uncontrived and elemental, and *Responses* derives its meaning from this impromptu tone as much as the content. In fact, the imitation of speech calls attention to a paradox in his project. If he had, as Chalupecký argued, abandoned the use of language for his poetry by the 1960s, why did he lean on it so heavily here? *Responses* offers no answers. It is merely another abrupt turn for an artist who was driven by reinvention. For this reason, *Responses* should not be read as Kolář's final word but as capturing a particular moment in time amid his creative flux.

R. S., PRAGUE, 2021

JIŘÍ KOLÁŘ (Protivín, 1914 – Prague, 2002) was one of the most important postwar poets/visual artists in Central Europe. A member of the avant-garde Group 42 (disbanded in 1948 following the Communist coup in Czechoslovakia), most of his major texts were composed in the 1950s and '60s. In 1952, he was arrested, jailed, and branded an "enemy of the state" when the secret police discovered the manuscript to his prose and poetry collection, *Prometheus's Liver*. He is, however, more well known internationally for his collage innovations, including his famous series *Weekly 1968*. He developed a number of techniques for combining and manipulating scraps of texts and images from a variety of sources to portray the destruction and fragmentation of the world around him, and by the 1970s his work was being exhibited throughout Europe. Kolář signed Charter 77, which put him in direct opposition to the Communist regime and ultimately forced him into exile. He lived in Paris from 1980, but frequently visited Prague after the Velvet Revolution in 1989, spending his final years in the city.

RYAN SCOTT is an Australian writer and translator based in the Czech Republic. His poetry, prose, and translations have appeared in a number of publications, including *Disquieting Muse Quarterly*, *B O D Y*, *Overland Express*, and *New England Review* (Australia). He is the translator of *A User's Manual* by Jiří Kolář.

RESPONSES • KAFKA'S PRAGUE
by Jiří Kolář

Translated by Ryan Scott from the original Czech
Odpovědi (Köln: Index, 1984)

Artwork by Jiří Kolář
German translations by Kevin Blahut
Typeset in Garamond Pro / Univers
Design by Silk Mountain

FIRST EDITION 2021

TWISTED SPOON PRESS
P.O. Box 21 – Preslova 21
150 00 Prague 5
Czech Republic
www.twistedspoon.com
twistedspoonpress@gmail.com

IMAGE TO WORD 6

Printed and bound in the Czech Republic
by Protisk

Distributed to the trade by

CENTRAL BOOKS
www.centralbooks.com

SCB DISTRIBUTORS
www.scbdistributors.com